Beyond Reality

SECOND EDITION

BEYOND REALITY

The Comprehensive Guide to Virtual and
Augmented Worlds

CAN BARTU H.

2024

Beyond Reality

Can Bartu H.

Preface

The fast evolution of generation is reshaping our perception of reality and our interplay with the sector round us. The barriers of the bodily global are increasingly mixing with the limitless possibilities provided by means of the digital realm. At the coronary heart of this variation lie technologies that bridge virtual environments with the bodily world, permitting seamless transitions among them. Today, we are able to explore nation-states past our creativeness, where digital and bodily realities converge in approaches we in no way thought possible.

This book delves into a comprehensive exploration of technology like virtual reality, augmented reality, and digital twins. It is written to manual the reader thru the profound modifications these technologies bring, not handiest to industries and groups however additionally to society, training, and the way we revel in the sector. From the theoretical foundations behind these technology to the modern packages that are shaping the prevailing and destiny, this book gives insights into how these technology are transforming our lives.

As virtual realities and virtual reviews become greater immersive and interactive, the opportunities they gift are big. Yet, along these advancements come demanding situations, particularly in terms of moral issues and societal effect. This ebook does not simply look at technological progress; it additionally reflects on the broader implications of those improvements. How will they reshape human interaction? What role do *ethics play on this rapidly evolving international? And how are we able to navigate those modifications while maintaining responsibility toward both the digital and bodily worlds?*

The goal here isn't always just to present technological progress, however to help the reader understand the creative, moral, and societal dimensions of those advancements. As we flow forward into this digital destiny, it's essential to don't forget how we can shape a international this is both revolutionary and sustainable. This adventure will not only explore the contemporary state of these technologies however will even have a look at how they are able to inspire new worlds, spark creativity, and pressure destiny exchange. Ultimately, this e-book hopes to function a guide to navigating and contributing to a digitalized world that is full of potential and opportunities.

CONTENTS

CHAPTER 1

What is Virtual Reality and Augmented Reality?

1.1. Virtual Reality and Augmented Reality Concepts

Virtual fact (VR) and augmented reality (AR) are not simply technological tendencies; they constitute a profound evolution in how human beings revel in, interpret, and have interaction with the sector round them. These ideas have transcended the bounds of enjoyment and entered the geographical regions of training, healthcare, layout, communication, and even our notion of lifestyles. At their center, both VR and AR cope with the fusion of virtual and bodily realities, albeit in distinctive ways. Understanding their fundamental differences and shared capacity is important for greedy the future trajectory of human-pc interplay.

Virtual truth may be understood as a totally immersive digital enjoy, wherein customers are positioned within a totally pc-generated environment. Through the use of head-hooked up shows and sensory system, individuals are visually and frequently bodily indifferent from the physical global and transported right into a digital area that is either a replication of reality or a very fantastical construct. In evaluation, augmented reality complements the real global by overlaying digital records onto the bodily environment. This is usually accomplished through gadgets like smartphones, capsules, or AR glasses that task digital factors onto what the consumer sees in real time.

While VR replaces reality with a digital realm, AR enriches it with additional records and visible layers.

The distinction in immersion among VR and AR defines the character of their use. VR's potential to fully have interaction the consumer's senses permits it to recreate eventualities that may be impossible, risky, or impractical in real life. It gives overall detachment, allowing customers to interact with simulations that call for entire consciousness and emotional presence. AR, through comparison, enhances the person's interaction with the real global by imparting contextualized facts, real-time instructions, and adaptive interfaces. This integration instead of substitution of fact permits AR to blend seamlessly into daily lifestyles, influencing fields consisting of navigation, faraway assistance, retail, and business diagnostics.

The emergence of VR and AR as wonderful however overlapping domains stems from the broader pursuit of spatial computing and embodied interplay. Both rely upon a complex integration of software, hardware, and cognitive technology. To simulate or augment fact convincingly, these systems ought to tune movement, render dynamic content material, and react in actual time to the consumer's actions and surroundings. The sophistication of those systems reflects a long time of studies in visible processing, human perception, and interface design. VR systems usually encompass positional monitoring, motion-sensing controllers, and auditory remarks mechanisms that enable users to have interaction obviously in the digital space. AR structures need to acquire accurate spatial mapping of the surroundings to region digital factors with contextual precision.

One of the most profound conceptual differences lies in how those technology impact human perception. VR rewires the user's feel of area, scale, and time by means of setting them into environments with their own internal good judgment. Users can revel in 0 gravity, walk at the floor of Mars, or navigate summary statistics structures as though they have been physical spaces. This sort of enjoy demanding situations traditional cognitive barriers, reshaping how users have interaction with facts and narratives. AR, then again, modifies perception through enriching the prevailing surroundings, making the invisible visible. It can reveal inner mechanical systems of machinery, simulate physiological processes on a human body, or overlay multilingual subtitles in live conversations. Both technologies push the bounds of notion however in divergent instructions—VR thru detachment and reinvention, AR thru augmentation and enhancement.

As these technology evolve, the difference among VR and AR begins to blur. Mixed reality (MR), frequently taken into consideration a continuum among VR and AR, allows virtual and real-global objects to coexist and engage in actual time. Devices together with Microsoft's HoloLens and Magic Leap's spatial computing platform exemplify this hybrid technique, merging immersive interplay with real-global focus.

This convergence indicates a shift from character, remoted reviews to shared, interactive environments that may respond to both the user and their environment. MR combines the immersion of VR with the contextual grounding of AR, imparting effective equipment for collaboration, training, layout, and remote paintings.

The development of VR and AR has prompted now not simplest technological innovation however additionally philosophical inquiry. These systems undertaking the traditional perception of what's actual, prompting a reevaluation of sensory trust and epistemological truth. In VR, customers willingly droop disbelief and receive the virtual assemble as temporarily actual. The brain translates those stimuli as true, often triggering emotional and physiological responses indistinguishable from those in the real global. AR continues the foundation of reality however overlays it with elements that could or may not be perceived by means of others. This shared-unshared dichotomy gives exciting questions on social notion, conversation, and the negotiation of that means in digitally augmented areas.

In both cases, the consumer's presence will become a dynamic interface. The potential to look around, circulate, talk, and manage objects alters the paradigm of passive intake into one in every of energetic participation. This interactivity transforms learning into exploration, storytelling into immersion, and selection-making into embodied cognition. VR users do no longer merely study—they input and affect. AR users do not just get admission to statistics—they experience it as an instantaneous extension of their physical surroundings. This shift redefines the consumer from a spectator to a co-creator, from a consumer to an agent inside the device.

The implications of these standards stretch past person enjoy to encompass societal transformation. In medication, VR is getting used to simulate complex surgical procedures, treat phobias, and rehabilitate neurological conditions through gamified sporting events. AR gives real-time visualizations for surgeons, improving precision and protection. In structure and urban planning, VR allows stakeholders to stroll through unbuilt spaces, changing their design based on experiential comments. AR provides layers of data to production websites, improving coordination and decreasing error. In schooling, both technology revolutionize pedagogy, permitting experiential gaining knowledge of that transcends the constraints of textbooks and school rooms. Students can discover the anatomy of the human frame, dissect digital frogs, or conduct chemistry experiments with out risk.

Entertainment and media have visible some of the earliest and most seen programs of VR and AR. From immersive VR games to interactive AR installations in museums, those technologies have grow to be tools for storytelling, engagement, and sensory stimulation. Cinematic stories are evolving into fully navigable narratives, where users have an effect on plotlines via their choices and interactions. Advertising and retail have also embraced AR, permitting customers to preview products in their houses, try on garb truly, or acquire contextual promotions primarily based on area and conduct.

In the place of job, VR and AR are reshaping collaboration and productivity. Virtual conferences in spatial environments reflect the dynamics of bodily presence, whilst AR programs support real-time steerage and troubleshooting in technical fields. Remote teams can interact with 3D models, discover digital prototypes, and make choices as though co-located. These skills are mainly widespread in a globalized international where physical presence is now not a given. The merging of spatial computing with cloud infrastructure and AI enables scalable, information-pushed interplay that transcends geographic constraints.

Despite their developing integration, challenges remain. Both VR and AR require sizeable computational electricity, specific tracking, and high-constancy rendering to supply convincing reports. Latency, decision, and motion sickness are ongoing technical issues. Ethical and psychological considerations are similarly pressing. The immersion offered through VR can blur the road among digital and actual, potentially leading to escapism or detachment from reality. AR's ability to regulate notion increases issues about surveillance, facts privacy, and manipulation of records. As these structures end up more pervasive, the need for ethical frameworks, transparency, and consumer manipulate turns into vital.

The mental impact of lengthy-term exposure to those technology is still being studied. Early research suggests that immersive VR can impact empathy, reminiscence, and identity. Users who embody avatars may internalize behaviors and attitudes associated with the ones representations, a phenomenon referred to as the Proteus effect. AR's regular overlay of records may affect interest, cognition, and social dynamics. The human brain, while remarkably adaptable, might also face new cognitive demands in environments in which the boundary among virtual and physical is fluid.

Nevertheless, the promise of VR and AR continues to drive innovation and creativeness. As interfaces evolve towards mind-pc integration, tactile comments, and eye-monitoring, the realism and intuitiveness of those reviews will deepen. Spatial audio, environmental simulation, and AI-pushed characters will create extra plausible and emotionally resonant digital worlds. Meanwhile, AR turns into extra ambient and context-conscious, seamlessly woven into everyday lifestyles thru wearable devices, clever surfaces, and neural interfaces.

Virtual fact and augmented reality aren't simply technological constructs—they're philosophical provocations, psychological experiments, and cultural catalysts. They offer new dimensions of revel in, creativity, and verbal exchange.

They project what it manner to be gift, to examine, to empathize, and to create. As we step past the constraints of bodily truth, we enter a new frontier where the imagination turns into a shared space, and wherein the limits between the real and the virtual are not traces to be drawn, however dimensions to be explored.

1.2. Historical Development: Origins of Virtual Reality and Augmented Reality

The roots of digital reality and augmented fact stretch a long way deeper into human records than the advent of virtual headsets and smartphones would possibly recommend. Long before those technologies obtained their contemporary definitions, the human creativeness laid the basis for immersive worlds. From historical philosophical inquiries into belief and illusion to the mechanical innovations of the Renaissance and the computational leaps of the 20th century, the conceptual framework for digital and augmented reviews has been constructed over centuries.

One can hint early glimmers of virtuality inside the allegorical stories of antiquity. Plato's "Allegory of the Cave" in The Republic turned into a foundational metaphor that raised questions on fact, phantasm, and perception — ideas that resonate deeply with the center of both digital and augmented technology. The notion that truth will be mediated or manipulated to present a model different from the bodily international was a provocative idea even in ancient instances.

Fast ahead to the Renaissance, and the emergence of attitude in art signaled a shift in how truth became represented and perceived. Artists like Leonardo da Vinci started out crafting scenes with mathematical accuracy that gave visitors a 3-dimensional sense inside a -dimensional area. Though missing the interactivity of today's systems, those works were arguably the first attempts to construct opportunity realities the use of tools of phantasm and immersion.

The 19th century noticed technological trends that further driven the bounds of perceived fact. The invention of the stereoscope in the 1830s by means of Charles Wheatstone allowed customers to view paired pictures with barely unique perspectives, developing a resounding illusion of depth. Later, in 1838, this concept became multiplied through David Brewster with a cultured version of the stereoscope that used lenses and mirrors — a generation that laid the basis for the visual good judgment utilized in VR headsets over a century later.

The 20th century marked a sizeable transition from theoretical and artistic representations of altered realities to the advent of actual systems capable of simulating them. One of the earliest mechanical examples came in 1929, when Edwin Link developed the Link Trainer, an electromechanical flight simulator used for pilot training for the duration of World War

II. Though now not immersive by using these days's requirements, it introduced the idea of simulating environments for practical purposes — a principle that maintains to underpin VR and AR applications in education and training.

By the 1960s, the conceptual and technological basis of virtual and augmented environments had matured enough to inspire greater state-of-the-art experiments. In 1962, Morton Heilig added the Sensorama, a multimodal system designed to supply an immersive cinematic enjoy. The tool combined 3-D visuals with stereo sound, vibrations, or even scent shipping, aiming to completely have interaction the person's senses. Around the same time, Heilig additionally filed a patent for the Telesphere Mask, an early head-set up show (HMD) that offered stereoscopic images and was a vital step toward the primary era of VR gear.

Another pivotal figure was Ivan Sutherland, frequently called the "father of laptop snap shots." In 1968, he developed the first head-hooked up show gadget, called the "Sword of Damocles" because of its large, ceiling-installed guide shape. This tool became able to rendering simple wireframe images that modified in response to the consumer's head moves — marking step one closer to actual-time interactive digital environments.

In parallel, the theoretical underpinning of augmented truth became evolving. The concept of masking virtual facts onto the bodily world turned into explored in early army and aviation programs, especially through heads-up presentations (HUDs). These structures had been to start with designed to undertaking critical flight information onto transparent displays inside the pilot's line of sight. Though primitive, HUDs introduced the core idea of augmenting real-world belief with extra layers of information.

The 1970s and 1980s saw a shift toward integrating laptop energy with immersive simulation. Universities and research labs commenced experimenting with pc-generated environments. One first-rate instance turned into the Aspen Movie Map, evolved at MIT within the past due 1970s. It allowed users to navigate thru a digital representation of Aspen, Colorado, using video facts and laptop interfaces — a forerunner to trendy interactive mapping equipment and virtual excursions.

As computing energy elevated in the 1980s and 1990s, the economic ability of VR and AR technology started to emerge. Jaron Lanier, founding father of VPL Research, have become a primary figure throughout this period. VPL developed some of the first commercially to be had VR system, such as the DataGlove and the EyePhone (a VR headset). These devices allowed users to have interaction with virtual environments the use of hand and head moves, paving the way for the user interface fashions we see today.

Meanwhile, AR continued to evolve along a parallel route, particularly in army, aerospace, and industrial sectors.

Boeing, for instance, commenced experimenting with the usage of head-established displays to help technicians in assembling complicated wiring harnesses. These early AR structures had been tethered to powerful computers and remained limited to laboratories or specialized environments, however they laid the technical foundation for later, extra available programs.

The 21st century brought a dramatic acceleration within the improvement of each VR and AR, fueled by the upward push of cellular computing, advanced sensors, and compact shows. The release of the first iPhone in 2007 added effective computing, motion sensors, and excessive-resolution displays into a unmarried hand held device. These additives would show crucial to destiny AR programs, which might use cellphone cameras and processors to interpret and augment physical environments in real time.

By 2012, Oculus Rift, a crowdfunded undertaking led by using Palmer Luckey, re-energized interest in digital reality with a promise of lower priced, brilliant immersion for consumers. Its achievement caught the attention of principal technology firms, leading to Facebook's acquisition of Oculus in 2014. This flow signaled the begin of a new generation, as corporations like Google, Microsoft, Sony, and Apple invested closely in both VR and AR ecosystems.

Microsoft's launch of HoloLens in 2016 delivered new sophistication to AR studies, permitting users to engage with 3-d holographic content anchored to actual-global spaces.

Google's ARCore and Apple's ARKit in addition multiplied the attain of AR by enabling builders to construct augmented applications at once into smartphones and capsules with out additional hardware.

Today, VR and AR technologies are no longer novelties or experimental gear. They are deployed throughout a wide spectrum of industries — from remedy and training to enjoyment, structure, retail, and protection. Their evolution from philosophical musings and mechanical illusions to digitally built realities represents a brilliant fusion of human creativity, technical innovation, and cultural transformation. As they continue to develop, the historic journey of those technologies serves as each a reminder of our capacity to reshape belief and a basis for future explorations into the character of truth itself.

1.3. Current Virtual Reality and Augmented Reality Technologies

The fast evolution of digital fact (VR) and augmented reality (AR) technologies in current years has converted these as soon as area of interest standards into mainstream tools, essentially altering how we engage with the digital global. From immersive VR environments that transport customers into completely new worlds to AR structures that overlay virtual content material onto the bodily world, those technology are reshaping diverse industries and applications, from amusement and training to healthcare and layout. As each VR and AR preserve to develop, the distinction among the digital and physical geographical regions is turning into increasingly more blurred.

The maximum seen and generally used VR era nowadays is the head-hooked up show (HMD), which immerses users in a completely digital environment. These devices are available various forms, from high-give up, tethered systems just like the Oculus Rift, HTC Vive, and PlayStation VR, to standalone headsets inclusive of the Oculus Quest. These systems use a mixture of sensors, such as accelerometers, gyroscopes, and optical monitoring, to music the person's head and frame moves, growing a dynamic and responsive enjoy. The high-decision monitors and superior optics inner these devices make certain that users understand an environment as though they're without a doubt a part of it, with a extensive field of view, stereoscopic intensity, and realistic lights outcomes.

Inside these VR environments, customers can have interaction with the environment the usage of specialised controllers or hand monitoring. The Oculus Touch controllers, as an instance, are extensively used for this motive, imparting the ability to control objects, gesture, and interact in immersive video games or simulations. In addition at hand controllers, movement capture structures and complete-frame tracking also are turning into increasingly more popular in VR setups, allowing for extra fluid and herbal interactions inside virtual areas. Technologies like haptic comments additionally play a essential role in VR immersion, offering tactile sensations that enhance realism — whether or not it's the sensation of retaining an item, receiving a gentle vibration, or experiencing a collision in a simulated environment.

Beyond the consumer-targeted VR structures, advanced VR technologies are being used in specialised fields which includes scientific education, architectural visualization, and clinical research. In healthcare, VR has become a precious device for surgical schooling, ache control, and rehabilitation. Surgeons can now exercise complex methods in a hazard-free virtual environment, at the same time as patients present process physical remedy can interact in VR-primarily based physical activities that motivate them and boost up recovery. Furthermore, VR is being utilized for mental health remedies, with healing simulations used to treat PTSD, tension problems, and phobias through managed publicity remedy.

Simultaneously, augmented fact (AR) technology has visible full-size improvements, in particular with the proliferation of smartphones and drugs ready with powerful processors and excellent cameras. The maximum familiar form of AR nowadays is in all likelihood the one skilled thru mobile gadgets, where apps like Pokémon GO and Snapchat filters overlay digital elements on the real-global environment thru the device's camera. However, the scope of AR is going a long way beyond those recreational packages.

Modern AR reports are powered by way of state-of-the-art technologies that allow actual-time interplay with the physical world. These systems rely on laptop imaginative and prescient and item recognition algorithms to recognize the environment, allowing digital content to be anchored in specific locations and to respond dynamically to the user's moves. For instance, AR apps can test a room and task 3D models of fixtures, letting users visualize how a new couch would possibly suit into their residing area before creating a purchase. Similarly, in industrial settings, AR can help technicians in complicated meeting or repair responsibilities via showing step-with the aid of-step commands and visible cues directly on the equipment they're operating on, guiding them through procedures in real time.

A super advancement in AR generation is the improvement of AR glasses and headsets. Companies like Microsoft and Magic Leap are at the forefront of this innovation, with products like the Microsoft HoloLens and Magic Leap One supplying palms-loose augmented reviews. These devices use a combination of cameras, sensors, and spatial mapping to challenge holographic photographs onto the user's environment, allowing them to have interaction with both the bodily international and the virtual overlay simultaneously. Unlike smartphone-based AR, those headsets provide a greater immersive enjoy, because the virtual content seems to exist within the physical area, rather than being viewed through a display screen.

In addition to cellular gadgets and glasses, AR generation is likewise making its way into smart touch lenses and other wearables. These gadgets promise to in addition integrate AR into every day life by means of eliminating the need for cumbersome headsets or smartphones, imparting a continuing, palms-loose enjoy. Research is ongoing into contact lenses with included presentations, which could at some point challenge digital information immediately onto the wearer's retina, blending the digital and physical worlds in unheard of approaches.

One of the maximum exciting trends in both VR and AR is using artificial intelligence (AI) to enhance user studies. AI is being included into VR and AR programs to create greater smart, adaptive environments. In VR, AI algorithms can help generate dynamic content, consisting of procedurally generated worlds or responsive non-participant characters (NPCs) that react to the person's actions. In AR, AI-powered object reputation and monitoring permit virtual content material to seamlessly have interaction with the actual world, even as AI can also beautify augmented reality via imparting real-time translations or contextual facts based on the consumer's surroundings.

Another extensive fashion is the upward push of 5G networks, which promise to dramatically decorate both VR and

AR reports. The ultra-fast speeds and occasional latency presented through 5G will allow actual-time streaming of first-rate virtual environments and allow extra responsive, interactive AR programs. This is in particular crucial for cloud-based totally VR and AR services, where the heavy processing load is offloaded to far flung servers, and the consumer's tool simply renders the streamed content. The extended bandwidth of 5G can even assist more complex and immersive experiences, making an allowance for more sensible and particular digital worlds that aren't confined through the limitations of local hardware.

As each VR and AR technology preserve to evolve, they're increasingly being integrated right into a extensive range of industries and programs. From immersive gaming and entertainment to far off collaboration, healthcare, education, and industrial layout, the ability of those technology to beautify human interaction with each digital and real environments is limitless. While challenges stay, consisting of enhancing hardware comfort and affordability, minimizing movement sickness, and increasing content material availability, the cutting-edge kingdom of VR and AR technologies represents a wonderful fulfillment and a glimpse into the future of human-pc interplay.

The transformation of the physical and digital worlds is well underway, with VR and AR leading the manner in growing greater immersive, interactive, and interconnected experiences.

With endured advancements in hardware, software program, and network infrastructure, the strains among the bodily and digital nation-states turns into increasingly more indistinguishable, paving the manner for brand spanking new opportunities in verbal exchange, creativity, and exploration.

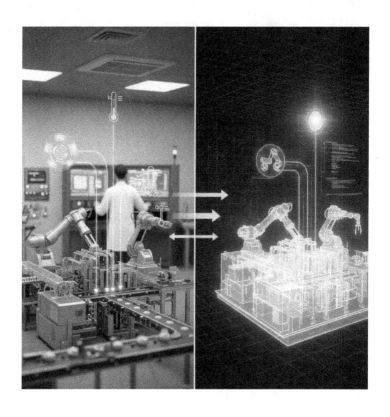

CHAPTER 2

Digital Twins: The Convergence of Real and Virtual Worlds

2.1. The Concept of Digital Twins

2.1.1. Origins of the Digital Twin Concept

The concept of virtual twins has evolved hastily in recent years, gaining prominence throughout industries because of its potential to bridge the space among the physical and virtual worlds. At its core, a digital dual refers to a digital illustration or duplicate of a physical entity, machine, or procedure. This digital counterpart is built from actual-time records amassed through sensors and different facts-gathering gadgets embedded within the bodily object, presenting an in depth and dynamic view of its behavior, performance, and circumstance. By the usage of a virtual twin, groups can simulate, analyze, and optimize actual-global strategies without having to bodily have interaction with the item, imparting a transformative approach to layout, protection, and operation.

The origins of the digital dual concept may be traced again to the aerospace industry, wherein the notion of creating a digital model of an aircraft or spacecraft became first explored in the early days of engineering and layout. However, it became not until the overdue 20th century that the term "virtual twin" started to take form inside the context we apprehend it today.

The roots of virtual twins are intently tied to the development of product lifecycle management (PLM) and pcaided design (CAD) structures. As manufacturing and engineering methods superior, engineers and designers started the use of digital models to symbolize physical items. These fashions have been initially used more often than not for the layout and prototyping degrees, allowing teams to visualise the object in a virtual space earlier than physical production started out. However, those early digital models have been static representations, and not using a real-time interaction with the physical item.

The leap forward in virtual twin generation came inside the 2000s while the concept turned into formally delivered by means of Dr. Michael Grieves, a professor on the University of Michigan, in 2002. In a presentation on the Society of Manufacturing Engineers, Grieves discussed the idea of a "virtual thread" — a virtual record of a product's design, manufacturing, and operational lifestyles. This virtual thread would connect all stages of a product's lifecycle, supplying a continuous flow of statistics from the bodily product to its digital twin. By linking the virtual and physical worlds, the virtual dual could provide a dynamic and real-time model of the product, supplying useful insights into its overall performance, wear, and operational efficiency.

Grieves' vision became especially groundbreaking as it recognized that a virtual twin became no longer only a static representation of a product, however a dynamic model that evolves alongside its bodily counterpart. As a product undergoes changes, studies wear and tear, or interacts with its surroundings, the virtual dual could reflect these adjustments in real time. This concept represented a prime shift from conventional methods, in which virtual models were simply used as design tools instead of lively, actual-time representations of bodily gadgets.

The virtual twin idea won in addition traction within the years that accompanied, as improvements in facts collection technologies, along with sensors, the Internet of Things (IoT), and cloud computing, made it possible to collect and transmit actual-time records from physical structures to virtual fashions. This enabled digital twins to transport beyond theoretical applications into sensible, actual-global makes use of.

One of the primary sizeable implementations of virtual twin era got here inside the aerospace and automobile industries. For instance, in 2011, NASA commenced the usage of virtual twins to simulate the overall performance of spacecraft at some stage in missions, permitting engineers to display structures in actual-time and modify operations if necessary. Similarly, in the automotive enterprise, manufacturers like BMW and General Motors started employing digital twins to display the performance of cars on the street, allowing them to predict maintenance wishes and enhance vehicle layout.

As the technology matured, virtual twins began to locate programs in a huge range of industries, which include manufacturing, energy, production, and healthcare. In manufacturing, virtual twins are used to optimize production lines, predict gadget failure, and improve deliver chain control. In power, they may be employed to monitor electricity grids, optimize energy consumption, and predict device disasters. In healthcare, digital twins are being explored for his or her capability in personalized medicine, in which a digital version of a affected person's frame could be used to expect the consequences of remedy or surgery.

The virtual twin idea has also received vast attention in the context of smart cities, in which digital twins are getting used to version and optimize urban infrastructure. These digital models allow town planners and authorities to simulate the effects of adjustments to infrastructure, consisting of the addition of recent buildings or the advent of latest transportation systems. This allows make sure that city improvement is efficient, sustainable, and aligned with the needs of the network.

Furthermore, the upward push of 5G networks and advancements in synthetic intelligence (AI) and device gaining knowledge of are poised to significantly beautify the talents of virtual twins. Real-time information series, analysis, and choice-making are predicted to emerge as even greater seamless and sensible, beginning up new opportunities for predictive maintenance, independent operations, and real-time optimization.

While the concept of digital twins has its origins in business and manufacturing contexts, it has quick turn out to be a go-disciplinary device with packages in a whole lot of fields. The convergence of the bodily and digital worlds through virtual twins is reshaping industries and allowing new innovations in product improvement, operation, and optimization. As the generation continues to evolve, the potential for virtual twins to convert not handiest man or woman industries however entire structures and societies is enormous. The digital twin is not just a theoretical idea; it's far unexpectedly turning into a cornerstone of the future of engineering, design, and operations.

2.1.2. Applications of Digital Twins within the Business World

The adoption of virtual twin generation has drastically transformed various industries, revolutionizing how groups perform, optimize, and innovate. Digital twins offer groups with the potential to create correct virtual models of their bodily belongings, methods, and systems, offering them a powerful device for real-time tracking, simulation, and predictive evaluation. These packages aren't only enhancing performance but also permitting businesses to make data-driven decisions that beautify productivity, reduce prices, and foster innovation. Across sectors inclusive of production, electricity, healthcare, retail, and logistics, digital twins are being leveraged to remedy complicated enterprise demanding situations and liberate new possibilities.

In the manufacturing industry, digital twins have come to be important for optimizing production traces, improving product first-class, and decreasing downtime. By growing a virtual replica of a manufacturing procedure, corporations can display the real-time overall performance of equipment, investigate the effectiveness of workflows, and identify capability issues before they result in highly-priced disruptions. Through predictive analytics, digital twins permit manufacturers to expect device screw ups, accordingly enabling proactive upkeep and reducing unscheduled downtime.

For example, General Electric (GE) makes use of digital dual technology in its aviation division to monitor jet engines. Each engine is paired with a digital dual that collects records from sensors embedded in the bodily engine, together with temperature, strain, and vibration. Engineers can then use this data to perform actual-time tracking and predictive protection, ensuring the engines are working at most advantageous efficiency. This technique has drastically reduced renovation costs and advanced the reliability and overall performance of aircraft engines.

In addition, virtual twins are being used to enhance the design and production of merchandise. By simulating the manufacturing system in a digital environment, manufacturers can optimize production sequences, reduce waste, and check one-of-a-kind configurations before committing to physical manufacturing. This capability not best shortens the time-to-marketplace but also enhances product first-rate and consistency.

Digital twins are also transforming deliver chain and logistics operations with the aid of providing greater visibility and control over the motion of products and inventory. By creating virtual twins of entire supply chains, companies can song and examine the glide of materials from providers to clients, optimizing stock tiers, lowering lead times, and identifying bottlenecks in the method.

One top notch software of digital twins in logistics is within the monitoring of delivery bins and cargo. Companies like Maersk and IBM are leveraging blockchain and IoT-enabled digital twins to track the motion of products throughout the globe. This allows businesses to gain real-time insights into stock levels, transport statuses, and capacity delays, allowing for better making plans and more efficient path optimization. Additionally, via using virtual twins to model whole supply chains, organizations can predict and mitigate risks related to supply chain disruptions, consisting of natural failures or geopolitical activities.

The potential to simulate various deliver chain scenarios with digital twins additionally enables companies to develop greater resilient logistics networks. By checking out the effect of various strategies, including changing suppliers or rerouting shipments, groups can prepare for unforeseen demanding situations and reply greater swiftly to changing market situations.

In the energy and utilities sector, digital twins are playing a pivotal position in optimizing operations, improving electricity performance, and reducing environmental affects. Power flowers, oil rigs, and renewable power farms are being equipped with digital twins to screen and manipulate the overall performance of essential infrastructure. By gathering real-time information on gadget overall performance, climate conditions, and strength production, operators can optimize the performance of strength era and distribution structures.

For example, Siemens Gamesa, a pacesetter in wind strength, makes use of virtual twins to simulate the performance of wind mills. By reading information accumulated from generators in actual time, engineers can expect whilst protection is needed, making sure that generators operate at top performance and reducing costly downtime. Similarly, oil and fuel organizations use virtual twins to monitor the overall performance of drilling device and pipelines, allowing them to are expecting capacity failures and prevent highly-priced accidents or environmental dangers.

Digital twins are also being employed to aid the transition to renewable strength sources. By simulating the performance of power structures and integrating facts from clever grids, utilities can optimize strength distribution, stability deliver and demand, and reduce energy wastage. In the context of smart cities, digital twins are used to model strength intake patterns, helping urban planners layout extra sustainable and strength-efficient infrastructure.

The healthcare sector is an increasing number of adopting virtual dual generation to improve affected person results, personalize treatment plans, and optimize health facility operations. By growing digital replicas of patients, medical gadgets, or complete healthcare systems, hospitals and healthcare providers can benefit deeper insights into affected person fitness, streamline operations, and improve the performance of care transport.

A massive software of digital twins in healthcare is the advent of personalised fashions of person sufferers. By integrating records from medical information, imaging structures, and wearable health devices, healthcare vendors can create a digital dual of a patient's frame to simulate and predict the consequences of various remedies. This permits medical doctors to tailor remedy plans to the specific needs of every patient, improving the effectiveness of interventions and minimizing risks. For example, a digital twin of a affected person's coronary heart will be used to predict the final results of different surgical processes or remedy regimens, supplying a greater specific and customized method to care.

In addition to affected person care, virtual twins are being used to optimize the control of healthcare facilities.

Hospitals are using virtual twins in their homes and equipment to display overall performance and count on renovation needs. By monitoring the condition of medical device, tracking affected person float, and simulating different care eventualities, healthcare carriers can enhance operational efficiency, lessen wait times, and improve the overall patient revel in.

In the retail sector, digital twins are being used to enhance customer stories and streamline operations. By developing virtual twins of shops, inventory structures, and consumer behaviors, outlets can examine shopping patterns, optimize shop layouts, and improve stock control. This enables outlets to create greater personalized buying experiences for customers and optimize product availability.

For example, virtual twins can simulate how a purchaser interacts with extraordinary shop layouts or product placements. This statistics may be used to design shop environments that maximize purchaser engagement and income. Additionally, retailers can use digital twins to optimize their deliver chains, making sure that the proper merchandise are available at the right locations and times to fulfill consumer call for.

The creation enterprise has additionally embraced virtual dual era for constructing design, production, and renovation. By creating virtual twins of production tasks, architects, engineers, and contractors can simulate building overall performance, stumble on design flaws, and optimize production workflows before any bodily work begins.

In the structure zone, digital twins are used to version homes and infrastructure in 3-d, permitting architects to visualise and optimize their designs. These virtual fashions can be tested for structural integrity, strength efficiency, and compliance with building codes, ensuring that the very last product meets the required requirements. During production, digital twins are used to track development, control resources, and make certain that the task stays on agenda.

After the building is completed, virtual twins hold to provide value through supporting the continued control and maintenance of the ability. By integrating sensors and IoT gadgets into the building, digital twins permit for actual-time monitoring of structures including HVAC, lighting fixtures, and security. This permits building managers to become aware of inefficiencies, predict renovation needs, and ensure that the constructing operates at height performance over its lifespan.

The applications of digital twins inside the enterprise international are enormous and preserve to extend as generation advances. From optimizing manufacturing strategies and deliver chains to enhancing healthcare consequences and improving purchaser reports, digital twins offer organizations a powerful device for improving performance, reducing prices, and fostering innovation. As the technology matures, it is probably that virtual twins turns into an crucial a part of every enterprise, using the destiny of enterprise operations and transforming the manner corporations interact with the physical international.

2.2. Alignment of the Real World and Digital Twins

The alignment of the actual global and digital twins is fundamental to the fulfillment and effectiveness of digital dual era. It involves the seamless integration of physical assets, systems, or strategies with their digital counterparts, bearing in mind actual-time records alternate, simulation, and predictive analysis. This alignment ensures that the digital dual accurately represents the bodily world, enabling corporations to reveal performance, make knowledgeable choices, and optimize operations. Achieving this alignment calls for the usage of superior sensors, Internet of Things (IoT) devices, records analytics, and device learning strategies to continuously feed statistics from the physical global into the digital version.

The foundation of aligning the real global with virtual twins is the continuous and correct acquisition of records. IoT sensors and devices positioned on physical assets, consisting of machinery, equipment, or vehicles, gather actual-time facts on various parameters, such as temperature, pressure, pace, and location. These sensors transmit this information to the digital twin, where it's far used to update the digital version, making sure that it reflects the modern-day kingdom of the physical asset or gadget.

For instance, in a manufacturing plant, machines ready with sensors provide information on their overall performance and condition. This records is sent to the virtual dual of the plant's manufacturing line, wherein it is used to simulate the manner and check its efficiency. If a machine is displaying symptoms of wear and tear or experiencing reduced performance, the virtual dual can alert operators, permitting them to schedule preservation earlier than a failure happens. This actual-time synchronization between the physical and digital worlds ensures that organizations can make proactive decisions and optimize their operations in actual time.

The alignment between the bodily global and virtual twins becomes greater accurate as the number of sensors and the nice of the records enhance. Advanced sensor technologies, inclusive of excessive-definition cameras, LiDAR, and radar, can seize designated and specific statistics from the bodily international, permitting virtual twins to represent complex environments with high fidelity. The accuracy of the facts being fed into the virtual twin at once impacts its capability to provide actionable insights, making high-quality information acquisition a key element of successful digital twin implementation.

One of the middle features of digital twins is to simulate the conduct of bodily structures in a virtual surroundings. This simulation calls for an accurate representation of the actual-world system, which is completed via the alignment of the physical and virtual worlds. By combining actual-time facts with superior modeling strategies, digital twins permit businesses to test situations, are expecting effects, and optimize strategies with out physically altering the structures.

In industries consisting of aerospace, virtual twins are used to version the overall performance of aircraft or spacecraft in a virtual surroundings. By aligning the virtual dual with information gathered from sensors at the physical car, engineers can simulate one of a kind flight situations, climate styles, and mechanical behaviors to optimize the layout and performance of the plane. This simulation helps identify potential issues, improve safety, and reduce development fees by way of testing and refining designs before physical prototypes are built.

Similarly, in city making plans, virtual twins of cities are created to model visitors flow, energy intake, and environmental factors. By aligning real-global information from site visitors cameras, sensors, and climate stations with the digital dual, metropolis planners can simulate how specific adjustments, inclusive of new roads or public transportation routes, will have an effect on the metropolis's infrastructure. This permits for better making plans and selection-making, making sure that city development is both green and sustainable.

One of the key advantages of aligning the actual international with virtual twins is the capacity to leverage predictive analytics. By constantly feeding actual-time facts from the bodily global into the virtual dual, companies can analyze tendencies, expect future behaviors, and make facts-pushed decisions. The virtual twin can use device gaining knowledge of algorithms and ancient information to become aware of patterns and forecast potential troubles, together with gadget screw ups, production delays, or supply chain disruptions.

For example, within the strength quarter, virtual twins of strength flora are used to expect whilst gadget would require preservation or while power call for will spike. By aligning real-time information on system performance and power consumption with the digital twin, operators can count on troubles before they stand up and take corrective motion. This predictive capability now not simplest reduces downtime but also facilitates optimize the usage of resources and enhance the overall performance of operations.

In the healthcare quarter, digital twins of patients are more and more used to are expecting the results of scientific remedies. By aligning statistics from medical gadgets, wearable fitness trackers, and patient facts with the digital dual, healthcare vendors can simulate the results of various treatments and expect their success. This alignment lets in for extra personalised remedy plans and better patient consequences by using tailoring interventions to the person desires of each patient.

In exercise, aligning the actual global with virtual twins has enabled many industries to unlock new degrees of efficiency, innovation, and sustainability. For example, in the car industry, digital twins of automobiles are created to display the fitness of man or woman additives, together with engines, brakes, and batteries. By aligning the data from the car's sensors with the digital twin, producers can identify put on and tear on parts and offer well timed protection or replacement, reducing the threat of breakdowns and lengthening the lifespan of the car.

Similarly, inside the production enterprise, virtual twins of production strains are used to align the bodily workflow with the digital model. Real-time statistics from machines, robots, and workers is fed into the digital twin to simulate and optimize the whole manufacturing procedure. This alignment lets in producers to become aware of inefficiencies, reduce waste, and improve the general throughput in their operations.

In agriculture, virtual twins are being used to model complete farms, aligning records from soil sensors, climate stations, and crop monitoring structures with the digital model. This alignment helps farmers optimize irrigation, monitor plant health, and are expecting crop yields, in the long run main to more efficient and sustainable farming practices.

As generation continues to conform, the alignment between the real world and digital twins turns into even more state-of-the-art. The integration of advanced technologies which includes 5G, side computing, and AI will enhance the real-time synchronization between physical property and their digital counterparts, allowing even extra accurate simulations, faster selection-making, and greater predictive skills.

In the close to destiny, using digital twins will expand beyond character property and systems to embody entire ecosystems, which includes smart cities or business clusters. By aligning data from a big range of sources, those massive-scale virtual twins will permit businesses and governments to manipulate complicated systems with unprecedented performance and perception.

The alignment of the real global and virtual twins is a important factor of the digital transformation manner. By ensuring that digital twins correctly reflect the physical international, companies can free up the entire potential of this generation, using innovation, enhancing performance, and optimizing operations throughout industries. As the era matures and information acquisition methods enhance, the alignment among the bodily and digital worlds will hold to deepen, main to new opportunities and talents that had been once unimaginable.

2.3. Application Areas of Digital Twins

Digital twins have come to be necessary to a huge range of industries, permitting organizations to bridge the distance between the physical and virtual geographical regions. By offering actual-time statistics, predictive insights, and the ability to simulate diverse eventualities, digital twins are revolutionizing operations throughout sectors such as production, healthcare, construction, energy, and urban planning. The good sized capability of digital twins spans numerous application areas, all of which leverage the dynamic and interactive nature of this technology. These packages no longer only streamline operations but additionally pave the way for brand new opportunities in the virtual transformation adventure.

In manufacturing, digital twins are used to duplicate production traces, machinery, and whole flora in a digital environment. By taking pictures actual-time facts from device, sensors, and structures, virtual twins offer an in depth, interactive illustration of the physical belongings. This allows operators to monitor the overall performance of machines and methods, discover faults early, and are expecting protection needs. Through non-stop facts streams, virtual twins help producers enhance performance, reduce downtime, and optimize manufacturing schedules.

One key utility is in predictive maintenance. With a virtual twin, producers can simulate the wear and tear of gadget through the years, become aware of whilst a system will require preservation, and agenda it in advance to keep away from sudden failures. This approach minimizes operational interruptions and lowers restore fees. Furthermore, digital twins allow for checking out of recent production approaches or modifications within the virtual surroundings, decreasing the risks and fees related to bodily trials.

Smart factories, equipped with interconnected machines and gadgets, are every other prominent instance of digital dual applications in manufacturing. These factories rely upon virtual twins to achieve better stages of automation, integration, and self-optimization. By reading facts from numerous machines, digital twins help producers decorate satisfactory manipulate, streamline workflows, and improve average operational overall performance.

The healthcare enterprise has embraced digital twins for their capability to simulate and monitor each character patients and medical devices. In patient care, a digital dual of a patient can be created by means of integrating information from diverse resources together with clinical facts, wearable gadgets, and sensors that music crucial symptoms. These virtual fashions provide healthcare specialists with personalized insights, letting them simulate treatments, display restoration, and predict the final results of clinical interventions.

For instance, digital twins are more and more used inside the control of persistent situations inclusive of diabetes or coronary heart disease. By constantly updating the digital dual with actual-time records from wearable fitness gadgets, docs can music a affected person's condition and make greater informed decisions about remedy. These digital fashions can also be used for checking out new capsules, methods, or remedy plans in a managed environment before making use of them to actual sufferers.

In the sector of scientific gadgets, virtual twins are used to monitor the overall performance of gadget like pacemakers, defibrillators, or MRI machines. By growing a digital twin of these gadgets, manufacturers can tune their overall performance, become aware of ability malfunctions, and time table maintenance for that reason. This is especially critical in excessive-chance clinical environments, in which gadget failure could have severe results.

The electricity and utilities area has been one of the early adopters of virtual dual era. In power era, virtual twins are used to version energy plants, wind farms, or solar energy structures, imparting operators with detailed insights into the performance of every asset. By continuously tracking real-time statistics from sensors placed on mills, sun panels, or other strength-generating components, digital twins can are expecting overall performance troubles, optimize energy output, and make sure the efficient operation of the plant.

For example, in wind energy, digital twins permit operators to simulate the overall performance of person generators below numerous weather situations, permitting predictive preservation and greater green power production. In the oil and gasoline enterprise, digital twins are applied to version pipelines, refineries, and garage tanks, making an allowance for actual-time monitoring and early detection of leaks or equipment malfunctions.

The implementation of virtual twins in the strength area additionally contributes to the transition toward more sustainable energy practices. By simulating electricity consumption and manufacturing, these digital fashions assist businesses lessen waste, optimize grid control, and improve the combination of renewable energy resources into the general electricity blend.

The creation and infrastructure sectors have seen sizable advancements because of the implementation of digital twins. In these fields, virtual twins are used to duplicate buildings, roads, bridges, and other infrastructure projects. They permit production groups, architects, and engineers to create accurate virtual models of a task earlier than production starts offevolved, improving layout accuracy and decreasing the chance of errors.

A key advantage of digital twins in construction is their capacity to simulate the entire lifecycle of a building or infrastructure assignment. From the planning and layout section to construction and eventual decommissioning, virtual twins help make sure that projects are finished on time, inside budget, and to specification. They enable actual-time tracking of construction development, presenting insights into ability delays, fee overruns, and safety issues.

Once completed, the digital twin of a building or infrastructure can continue to offer fee throughout its operational life. Building control systems, prepared with sensors that reveal temperature, humidity, lighting, and power usage, feed facts into the digital dual, allowing facility managers to optimize operations and improve strength performance. These virtual models also allow predictive maintenance, assisting to identify when additives, including HVAC systems or elevators, want servicing before they fail.

The automotive and aerospace industries are at the vanguard of virtual dual generation, where the ability to model complex systems in virtual environments plays a essential role in optimizing performance and ensuring protection. In automobile layout and manufacturing, digital twins reflect complete motors or man or woman additives, allowing manufacturers to check overall performance, evaluate new designs, and simulate how vehicles or trucks will behave in diverse conditions before manufacturing starts offevolved.

In aerospace, digital twins are used to simulate the performance of aircraft and spacecraft, ensuring that designs meet stringent safety and efficiency requirements. By growing a digital duplicate of an plane, engineers can test various flight conditions, pick out capability risks, and optimize the layout for gas performance and protection. This is in particular crucial for the improvement of subsequent-era aircraft, wherein digital twins assist streamline layout procedures and reduce the number of physical prototypes needed for testing.

The use of virtual twins in both the automotive and aerospace industries extends to maintenance and operational optimization. By monitoring real-time statistics from automobile sensors, digital twins allow predictive protection, figuring out issues earlier than they result in highly-priced maintenance or protection incidents.

One of the maximum promising packages of digital twins is within the development of smart cities. By creating virtual twins of entire cities, urban planners can simulate the results of diverse development projects, consisting of new transportation structures, energy infrastructure, or housing developments. These digital models allow for better decision-making, helping to optimize land use, improve site visitors management, and decrease environmental effect.

Digital twins are used to version town infrastructure, from roads and utilities to homes and transportation networks. By integrating records from IoT sensors, site visitors cameras, and weather stations, city planners can display actual-time situations, such as visitors float, air pleasant, and strength intake. This facts-pushed technique helps to create extra green, sustainable, and livable towns.

In the context of emergency control, digital twins can be used to simulate herbal disasters, which includes earthquakes or floods, and predict their impact on metropolis infrastructure. By checking out special emergency response techniques in a virtual environment, planners can pick out the best direction of motion to minimize damage and make sure public safety.

The agriculture industry has additionally benefited from using virtual twins. By developing digital models of farms, plants, and cattle, digital twins assist farmers optimize their operations, increase yields, and reduce waste. These fashions integrate information from soil sensors, weather stations, and crop-tracking gadgets to provide real-time insights into soil health, irrigation wishes, and pest control.

Farmers can use virtual twins to simulate extraordinary agricultural eventualities, together with crop rotations, fertilization schedules, or irrigation techniques. By testing those scenarios in a virtual environment, farmers can become aware of the simplest practices and make information-pushed selections that enhance sustainability and productivity.

Digital twins are also used in precision agriculture, in which drones and self reliant motors are deployed to screen plants and soil situations. These digital fashions allow farmers to stumble on potential troubles, including pest infestations or nutrient deficiencies, before they turn out to be tremendous, taking into consideration greater focused interventions.

The utility areas of virtual twins are considerable and retain to amplify as era advances. From production and healthcare to electricity, production, and agriculture, digital twins are reworking industries via supplying real-time insights, enhancing efficiency, and enabling predictive selection-making. As virtual twin era evolves, its effect will only develop, imparting new opportunities for innovation and optimization throughout the global economic system.

CHAPTER 3

Virtual Reality Experiences

3.1. Virtual Reality Headsets and Equipment

Virtual Reality (VR) has grow to be one of the maximum transformative technology of the cutting-edge era, allowing customers to immerse themselves in fully interactive digital environments. The center of this immersive revel in is the hardware used to deliver digital reality, mainly VR headsets and assisting equipment. These devices are essential in bridging the space among the bodily international and the digital realm, imparting users with the sensory enter required to create an immersive experience.

The journey of VR headsets commenced as early as the 1960s, however it wasn't until the 1990s that the generation started to seize huge attention, especially within the leisure industry. Early VR systems have been bulky and required a giant array of equipment, such as external monitoring gadgets and high-powered computer systems, making them impractical for regular use. However, the fast development of computing electricity, display technologies, and sensor structures within the 21st century has caused the development of headsets which are now greater low-cost, portable, and handy than ever earlier than.

In the early days, VR headsets used CRT (cathode ray tube) displays that have been heavy and occasional in decision. The first exquisite VR headsets, along with the Sega VR and the Virtual Boy by using Nintendo, were advertised to clients but failed because of technical barriers like low body quotes, negative resolution, and confined content material. These early models, at the same time as groundbreaking for their time, laid the foundation for more advanced headsets that would emerge later.

Today's VR headsets have superior significantly, with upgrades in show decision, processing electricity, and ergonomics. The integration of OLED (natural mild-emitting diode) and LCD (liquid crystal show) technologies has appreciably enhanced the visible revel in, imparting sharper snap shots and richer shades. Additionally, the development of higher refresh rates and stepped forward latency has made VR experiences greater fluid and responsive, lowering movement sickness and improving person comfort.

Modern VR headsets come with several key features that define the immersive experience. These functions consist of excessive-resolution displays, wide fields of view, low-latency tracking, and precise movement detection.

1. High-Resolution Displays: One of the most vital factors inside the fine of the virtual experience is the show resolution. Higher resolution presentations lessen the "display door impact," wherein users can see the grid of pixels at the display screen. Today's VR headsets typically offer resolutions that range from 1080p (according to eye) to 4K and even 8K

shows. This higher pixel density improves the sharpness and realism of virtual environments.

2. Wide Field of View (FOV): The subject of view refers back to the region seen through the VR headset. A wider FOV creates a greater immersive revel in by using making the digital world experience more expansive. The human eye has a natural FOV of about 210 degrees horizontally, however maximum VR headsets today provide an FOV of round 100 to 110 ranges, which is taken into consideration a candy spot for immersion.

3. Tracking and Latency: For VR to sense actual, head and hand movements should be tracked in actual-time, with minimal delay. Latency, or the delay among the consumer's motion and the corresponding alternate within the digital international, must be as low as possible to avoid pain or disorientation. Modern VR headsets appoint numerous monitoring structures, including inside-out tracking (wherein cameras at the headset tune the surroundings), or outside sensors placed around the play location.

4. Comfort and Ergonomics: Since users may additionally wear VR headsets for extended intervals, comfort is critical. Many VR headsets are designed with adjustable straps, foam padding, and lightweight materials to distribute the weight calmly and reduce pressure on the pinnacle. Features like adjustable interpupillary distance (IPD) ensure that the

lenses align well with the person's eyes for the exceptional viewing enjoy.

5. Built-in Audio: Immersive audio is critical to growing a convincing virtual surroundings. Many VR headsets now come with incorporated headphones or spatial audio technology that offer 3-d sound, enhancing the sense of presence. Headphones with noise cancellation also assist block out the actual-world environment, contributing further to immersion.

There are numerous famous VR headsets on the market these days, every catering to one of a kind person needs and budgets. These headsets vary in phrases of platform compatibility, overall performance, and supposed use, however all proportion the purpose of presenting a compelling digital fact experience.

1. Oculus Quest 2: Oculus, now owned through Meta (previously Facebook), has revolutionized VR with its wireless headsets. The Oculus Quest 2 is one of the most popular purchaser-degree VR headsets, recognised for its portability, ease of use, and relatively low-cost charge. It gives standalone operation without the need for a PC or external sensors, making it one of the maximum on hand VR headsets for beginners. The Quest 2 helps both wi-fi VR experiences and PC VR gaming when linked to a well suited pc thru a cable or Air Link for wi-fi play.

2. PlayStation VR (PSVR): Sony's PlayStation VR, designed to be used with the PlayStation console, has received full-size traction inside the gaming community. Although it's far tethered to a PlayStation 4 or PlayStation 5, it gives a stable VR experience with video games optimized for the device. With the imminent PlayStation VR2, Sony pursuits to enhance the visible constancy, tracking capabilities, and comfort of the headset, positioning it as a key player inside the gaming VR area.

3. Valve Index: Valve's Index headset is a premium choice for VR enthusiasts and game enthusiasts. Known for its terrific visible readability, excessive refresh rate (as much as 144 Hz), and particular finger-monitoring controllers, the Valve Index is often taken into consideration one of the exceptional VR structures for PC gaming. However, it requires a effective gaming PC and outside sensors for monitoring, that can restriction its accessibility.

4. HTC Vive Pro 2: HTC has been a leading participant in the VR market for years with its Vive collection. The Vive Pro 2 offers first rate decision (5K), high refresh charges, and correct monitoring, making it a pinnacle desire for experts and high-give up VR customers. Like the Valve Index, it calls for a PC connection and outside base stations for monitoring, however it offers a top rate enjoy for users who call for top-tier performance.

5. Microsoft HoloLens 2: While broadly speaking designed for combined reality (MR), Microsoft's HoloLens 2 carries elements of VR generation. Unlike traditional VR headsets, the HoloLens 2 overlays digital content onto the real international as opposed to replacing it absolutely. It is particularly popular in enterprise and business programs, in which it aids in tasks like education, remote help, and design visualization.

While the headset is the principal piece of gadget, several peripherals and accessories enhance the general VR enjoy. These encompass movement controllers, haptic feedback devices, and external sensors.

1. Motion Controllers: These hand-held devices are used to have interaction with the virtual global, supplying users with the potential to control items, navigate environments, and engage with content. Most VR systems use motion controllers that song the user's hand movements through sensors and cameras, providing a greater immersive and intuitive experience.

2. Haptic Feedback: Some VR setups consist of haptic feedback gadgets, consisting of vests, gloves, or suits, that offer tactile sensations, similarly improving immersion. These devices permit users to feel digital sensations, along with the impact of a virtual item or environmental changes like wind or temperature, growing a greater practical enjoy.

3. External Sensors: For greater advanced VR systems, outside sensors located across the play vicinity help tune the user's movements and make sure particular spatial attention. These sensors make a contribution to a smoother and extra correct revel in through lowering lag and improving positional monitoring.

Virtual fact headsets and supporting device shape the inspiration of immersive digital experiences. As generation continues to conform, those gadgets have become extra superior, offering better-exceptional visuals, extra correct monitoring, and extra consolation. Whether for gaming, training, enjoyment, or expert packages, VR headsets are vital to unlocking the full capability of digital reality, transforming the manner users have interaction with virtual environments and expanding the possibilities of what may be executed inside digital worlds.

3.2. Virtual Reality Games and Entertainment

Virtual Reality (VR) has significantly revolutionized the gaming and entertainment industries, offering an entirely new level of immersion that traditional media could never achieve. Through VR, users are no longer mere observers of a story or game but active participants, fully immersed in the worlds they inhabit. This shift from traditional flat-screen entertainment to a fully interactive 3D experience has not only reshaped the way we play games but has also redefined entertainment itself.

The concept of VR in gaming dates back to the early 1990s when companies like Sega and Nintendo attempted to create VR gaming systems. However, due to the technological limitations at the time, these attempts were not successful, resulting in VR gaming remaining more of a niche concept for many years. It wasn't until the 2010s, with the advent of more advanced computing power and immersive hardware, that VR gaming began to enter the mainstream. The development of powerful and affordable VR headsets, such as the Oculus Rift and HTC Vive, combined with improvements in graphics and tracking technology, helped bridge the gap between early concepts and current VR gaming experiences.

One of the key factors that made VR games more accessible to a broader audience was the release of standalone VR headsets like the Oculus Quest. This innovation allowed users to experience immersive gaming without the need for a high-end gaming PC or external sensors, removing many of the barriers to entry and making VR gaming more affordable and user-friendly.

Virtual reality introduces a paradigm shift in how games are designed. Traditional video games rely on visual feedback from a screen, but VR games involve the player's entire body, using head, hand, and sometimes even body movements to control the game world. This immersive gameplay requires a redesign of not only how games are controlled but also how they are structured.

In VR, the interaction with the virtual environment feels far more natural. For example, in a first-person shooter game, players can physically aim their weapons by moving their heads or hands, instead of simply pressing buttons or using a joystick. Similarly, in exploration-based games, players can look around their environment as if they are truly standing in that world, with a 360-degree field of view that is only possible in VR.

The increased sense of immersion has given rise to entirely new genres of games. Role-playing games (RPGs) and adventure games, where exploration and interaction are key components, benefit the most from the immersive qualities of VR. These games place the player in vast, rich worlds that feel as real as the physical world, allowing them to interact with characters, solve puzzles, and engage in complex scenarios that wouldn't be possible with traditional gaming interfaces.

Key VR Game Genres

1. First-Person Shooters (FPS): FPS games in VR are one of the most popular genres, offering fast-paced, action-packed gameplay. The addition of physical movement and aiming with hand controllers makes these games more engaging and interactive. Titles like Half-Life: Alyx and Superhot VR have become iconic examples of VR FPS experiences, offering players unprecedented immersion and realism in the world of virtual combat.

2. Puzzle and Adventure Games: The puzzle and adventure genre is particularly suited for VR, as players can use their hands to manipulate objects in the virtual world. Games like The Room VR and Myst allow players to explore intricate, visually stunning worlds, solve puzzles, and interact with objects in ways that traditional games cannot replicate. These games emphasize exploration and critical thinking, making them a hit for users looking for a more cerebral and immersive experience.

3. Simulations: VR's ability to simulate real-world environments has made it incredibly popular in genres such as flight simulators, car racing, and even sports. Games like Microsoft Flight Simulator VR and Dirt Rally VR let users experience highly realistic versions of real-world activities. Simulations in VR can feel incredibly lifelike, providing a level of realism and immersion not seen in traditional gaming.

4. Survival and Horror Games: The fear and tension that are core components of survival and horror games are magnified in virtual reality. The ability to look around and physically move within a game world adds a layer of anxiety and excitement that standard horror games cannot match. Titles such as Resident Evil 7 VR and The Walking Dead: Saints & Sinners leverage VR's immersive nature to create truly terrifying experiences that make players feel like they are living within the horror themselves.

5. Fitness and Exercise Games: VR has also carved a niche in the fitness industry, with games designed to get players moving and engaging in physical activity. Games like Beat Saber and BoxVR combine fun, rhythm-based gameplay with physical exercise, providing a unique way to work out. By incorporating full-body motion tracking, VR fitness games give players a sense of immersion that encourages movement and physical exertion, making them popular choices for health-conscious players.

Popular VR Games

Several titles have stood out as defining experiences in VR gaming, each showcasing the potential of the medium. These games are widely regarded as examples of what VR gaming can offer in terms of immersion, gameplay, and creativity.

• Half-Life: Alyx: Often hailed as one of the best VR games to date, Half-Life: Alyx takes full advantage of the immersive capabilities of VR. Set in the Half-Life universe, this first-person shooter puts players in the shoes of Alyx Vance as she fights to survive in a world overtaken by alien invaders. The game combines intricate environmental puzzles, intense combat, and a gripping story, all while making use of VR's natural interactivity to enhance immersion.

• Superhot VR: This innovative first-person shooter turns the concept of time into a key mechanic. In Superhot VR, time only moves when you move, allowing players to strategically plan each of their actions. This creates a unique puzzle-solving experience where players must think in slow motion and plan their movements carefully. The game's minimalist style and tactical gameplay have made it a favorite in the VR gaming community.

• Beat Saber: One of the most successful VR games to date, Beat Saber combines rhythm-based gameplay with full-body movement. Players use lightsabers to slice through blocks that are synchronized to the beat of the music. The game is fun, physically engaging, and perfect for players looking for an interactive way to enjoy music while also getting a workout.

• The Walking Dead: Saints & Sinners: This survival horror game puts players in a post-apocalyptic world filled with zombies. Players must scavenge for resources, build weapons, and survive in a world full of danger. The game is notable for its realistic physics, detailed world-building, and intense atmosphere, making it one of the most terrifying VR experiences available.

• Rec Room: Rec Room is a social VR platform that features a variety of games and activities, including sports, puzzles, and team-based challenges. Players can socialize with others, take part in mini-games, and explore creative spaces in a virtual world. Its social features make it a popular VR title, allowing players to interact with others in a shared environment.

As VR hardware continues to improve, the possibilities for VR games and entertainment will continue to expand. The development of new technologies, such as advanced AI, haptic feedback, and improved motion capture, will allow game developers to create even more realistic and interactive virtual worlds. Additionally, the rise of cloud gaming platforms, which allow users to stream games without the need for powerful hardware, may further lower the barriers to entry for VR gaming.

The future of VR entertainment also includes a growing interest in VR cinema and interactive storytelling. Filmmakers and game developers are experimenting with new ways of telling stories that place the viewer in the middle of the action. These immersive experiences will offer entirely new forms of entertainment, where the audience not only watches the story unfold but actively participates in shaping the narrative.

VR has already made significant strides in revolutionizing games and entertainment, and its potential is only just beginning to be realized. As technology continues to evolve, we can expect to see even more creative and innovative applications of VR, providing users with unparalleled immersion and new forms of interactive entertainment. The future of VR gaming holds exciting possibilities, promising a new era of entertainment where the lines between the virtual and real worlds continue to blur.

3.3. Virtual Reality and Education

Virtual Reality (VR) has more and more end up a effective device in schooling, reworking traditional teaching strategies and beginning new pathways for interactive and immersive gaining knowledge of stories. By offering a level of engagement and interactivity that textbooks and conventional media can not, VR permits college students to explore complicated subjects in approaches that have been previously inconceivable. This immersive era is not just about including a new size to getting to know but reshaping the entire educational enjoy.

One of the maximum considerable benefits of VR in schooling is its potential to create absolutely immersive environments that allow college students to engage at once with the challenge be counted. In traditional schooling, college students regularly analyze abstract ideas via studying or looking movies, which can be passive reports. VR adjustments this dynamic by using putting college students in an interactive 3-d area wherein they are able to explore, manage, and experiment with concepts in a palms-on way. This immersion promotes energetic mastering, wherein students are not simply passive recipients of data but lively contributors of their instructional journey.

For example, in a history lesson, in place of reading approximately historic Rome, students can enjoy on foot thru the streets of the Roman Empire, journeying landmarks, or interacting with historical figures. In technological know-how training, college students can explore the human anatomy from the interior or conduct digital chemistry experiments without the restrictions of bodily resources. The fingers-on, experiential nature of VR permits college students to keep knowledge higher, as they may be engaging with the content material on a couple of levels—visual, auditory, and tactile.

One of the maximum interesting applications of VR in schooling is the capability to take digital discipline journeys to locations that could otherwise be difficult or not possible to visit. Students can journey to historic websites, explore outer space, or even dive to the bottom of the ocean—all from the comfort in their school rooms. These virtual trips offer a feel of presence and area that no video or textbook can healthy. By moving into these digital worlds, college students can explore, research, and have interaction with their surroundings in real-time, making the enjoy a ways greater memorable and impactful.

Beyond discipline journeys, VR additionally lets in for actual-world simulations, where students can practice talents in a risk-free surroundings. For example, scientific college students can carry out surgeries using digital equipment and environments, presenting them with precious enjoy before ever working with real sufferers. Similarly, engineering students can layout and test prototypes in a virtual lab, helping them recognize the outcomes of their decisions without the fees and risks related to bodily experiments. These simulations provide a secure space for students to learn from mistakes, experiment with special tactics, and advantage self belief earlier than stepping into the actual world.

Another large benefit of VR in training is its potential to foster collaboration amongst students from specific geographical locations. Virtual school rooms, meeting spaces, and shared environments permit college students to have interaction with peers, instructors, and experts from around the arena. This global connectivity is in particular beneficial for college students in remote or underserved areas who might not have get admission to to awesome schooling or specialized instructors.

Through VR, students can take part in institution activities, along with problem-fixing obligations, crew projects, or stay discussions, as though they have been physically gift with one another. This fosters collaboration, vital questioning, and verbal exchange abilties which are critical in the contemporary international. For example, college students from one-of-a-kind international locations can collaborate on a international environmental task, gaining treasured insights into special cultural views and solutions.

Furthermore, VR allows students to have interaction with professionals and mentors from various fields in a manner that changed into as soon as reserved for in-character meetings or lectures. Imagine a scholar in a far flung village in Africa truly attending a seminar hosted by using a scientist in Europe or participating with a marine biologist in Australia. These opportunities open doors to a wealth of know-how and information that students can also never have had get admission to to otherwise.

VR additionally has the ability to tailor learning reports to person college students' desires. By the usage of information analytics and adaptive learning technology, VR systems can check a pupil's development, strengths, and weaknesses, adjusting the mastering experience thus. This customized approach ensures that each pupil is challenged at the proper level and might development at their very own pace, taking into account extra effective mastering results.

For students who warfare with conventional study room learning, VR can offer opportunity ways to apprehend and interact with complicated subjects. For example, a scholar with studying disabilities can also benefit from a more hands-on, visual getting to know experience, which VR can provide. VR also can be used to create environments where students can get hold of extra aid, which include virtual tutors or guided practice periods, with out the want for steady trainer intervention.

Certain fields of examine are specifically nicely-perfect for VR integration because of the complicated, fingers-on nature of the problem count number. These areas include medication, engineering, architecture, and the humanities. VR permits students in these fields to simulate actual-lifestyles eventualities and exercise their talents in a controlled and repeatable environment.

• Medicine and Healthcare: Medical college students can practice surgeries, diagnose sufferers, and explore human anatomy in methods that traditional schooling methods can't provide. VR can provide immersive, exact anatomical models that students can have interaction with, helping them recognize the human frame on a deeper level. Furthermore, VR simulations permit students to perform surgeries or clinical processes in a hazard-unfastened environment, giving them priceless practice earlier than managing real-life patients.

• Engineering and Architecture: In engineering and architecture, VR enables students to visualise complex designs and systems in 3-D. Instead of relying on blueprints or 2D fashions, students can step into their designs and walk via them, supplying a much extra intuitive know-how of area and shape. This immersive approach allows students become aware of capability issues, explore one-of-a-kind answers, and improve their layout abilities.

• Arts and Creativity: VR is likewise making its mark inside the innovative arts. In fields like digital artwork, animation, and recreation design, VR lets in college students to create and engage with their own virtual environments, generating 3D artwork that may be experienced from all angles.

Artists can use VR tools to sculpt, paint, and layout in digital space, expanding the possibilities of their creative expression.

Despite the numerous advantages of VR in training, numerous challenges continue to be. The fee of exquisite VR hardware and software program can be prohibitive for schools, specially in underfunded regions. The need for specialized training for each teachers and students to effectively use VR era also can be a barrier to significant adoption. Additionally, there are issues about the potential fitness consequences of prolonged VR use, which include eye strain, motion sickness, and physical discomfort.

To cope with these issues, colleges and educators should carefully remember the implementation of VR, ensuring that it is used as a supplement to traditional coaching techniques instead of a complete substitute. With the proper balance, VR can decorate schooling without overwhelming college students or educators with technical needs.

The integration of Virtual Reality into education is changing the manner we analyze, offering immersive, interactive, and personalized stories that traditional teaching methods can't offer. By breaking down the bounds of the study room and allowing students to revel in schooling in a extra engaging and fingers-on manner, VR has the ability to revolutionize the academic landscape. As generation keeps to adapt and grow to be extra on hand, the use of VR in education is in all likelihood to increase, paving the way for a future wherein getting to know is extra dynamic, worldwide, and tailor-made to the desires of each character scholar.

3.4. Travel and Exploration with Virtual Reality

Virtual Reality (VR) has dramatically reshaped the way we understand and engage with tour and exploration. Traditionally, journey turned into a physical interest, requiring resources, time, and the capacity to bodily shipping oneself to remote lands. With the appearance of VR, these conventional obstacles were lifted, opening up opportunities for virtual journeys that offer new styles of experiences. Now, individuals can explore the sector and even mission past the planet— without leaving their homes.

One of the most instant packages of VR inside the journey and exploration enterprise is the idea of virtual tourism. With VR headsets and immersive environments, customers can go to destinations across the globe from the comfort in their own dwelling rooms. This technology permits humans to discover iconic landmarks, ancient web sites, and natural wonders without the need for costly flights, time commitments, or bodily exertion.

Imagine stepping inside the Great Pyramids of Egypt, exploring the vibrant streets of Tokyo, or hiking to the height of Mount Everest—all through the lens of a VR headset. These virtual studies mirror the visible and auditory elements of journey, allowing customers to experience as even though they are bodily found in those remote locations. The added advantage of VR tour is the capacity to revel in environments that may be difficult, highly-priced, or risky to go to in actual lifestyles. For example, customers can now simply stroll through historic ruins, visit disaster-stricken areas, or discover the depths of the ocean, all in a safe and on hand manner.

Beyond Earth, VR is playing an vital position in area exploration and extraterrestrial tour. For decades, space tour has been restrained to a pick group of astronauts and scientists, with the general public best able to revel in space via documentaries or media reviews. However, VR era is now bridging this gap, supplying the general public a danger to revel in area exploration firsthand.

Virtual reality can simulate area missions, allowing users to experience what it seems like to tour via space, land at the moon, or maybe journey to Mars. By the usage of information and pics accrued by using area corporations like NASA, VR applications can mirror the environment of outer area with stunning accuracy. This opens up the opportunity of exploring distant planets, moons, and different celestial our bodies without the high price and complexity of actual-international area travel.

For example, VR structures can recreate the revel in of taking walks on the moon, supplying users the possibility to experience the low gravity, desolate terrain, and stark beauty of the lunar floor. Similarly, VR can provide distinctive visualizations of different planets in our sun gadget or distant galaxies, permitting human beings to look and interact with area as never before.

In addition to geographical travel, VR is remodeling how we revel in and understand cultures and records. Virtual truth can immerse customers inside the historic context of well-known occasions or convey long-long past civilizations to life. Users can in reality attend activities just like the signing of the Declaration of Independence or stand in the midst of a Renaissance-technology portray being created. VR lets in for a level of immersion that textbooks and documentaries can simplest advocate.

Virtual cultural exploration extends past historical activities to the modern-day-day realities of other areas. For instance, VR can take users to the bustling marketplaces of Morocco or the serene temples of Japan, presenting a deeper understanding of the lifestyle, customs, and every day exercises of human beings in different components of the arena. The ability to experience cultures in a multi-sensory way—by listening to the sounds of a hectic metropolis, tasting digital food, or attractive with nearby customs—creates a greater holistic enjoy than ever before.

For the ones unable to journey because of physical disabilities, economic constraints, or different barriers, VR journey affords a precious possibility to engage with the world in a significant and enriching manner. These immersive studies can encourage individuals to analyze extra approximately one of a kind cultures, records, and geography, fostering a experience of global connectedness and empathy.

While VR is revolutionizing journey for individuals, it is also impacting the journey enterprise itself. Tourism organizations are increasingly more incorporating VR technology into their marketing techniques, providing capacity customers with a flavor of destinations earlier than they book their trips. Hotels, motels, and airlines are offering VR tours that allow tourists to explore centers, destinations, or services earlier.

By the usage of VR to exhibit their services, organizations are growing extra enticing and informative ways for consumers to make tour choices. Instead of relying solely on brochures or websites, VR enables travelers to walk through a resort room, revel in the view from a cruise ship balcony, or take a guided tour of a traveler enchantment from a faraway place. This immersive preview can enhance the selection-making method, giving customers a clearer picture of what to expect from their travel reports.

Moreover, VR era is getting used to sell lesser-recognised locations and sights. By offering virtual experiences of off-the-overwhelmed-path locales, tourism forums and travel agencies can spark curiosity and interest in areas that vacationers won't have considered otherwise. This allows to diversify tourism and unfold the economic blessings of journey to regions that might otherwise war to draw worldwide visitors.

In addition to amusement and tourism, VR is likewise getting used for training and professional education in the fields of tour and exploration. Travel specialists, which includes tour publications, hospitality workers, and adventure instructors, can use VR to simulate real-global situations and enhance their abilities in a secure and managed surroundings. For example, a excursion manual can exercise main a group through a digital version of a popular vacationer website, gaining valuable enjoy earlier than guiding real travelers.

Similarly, VR is being employed in conservation efforts to help educate individuals on environmental preservation and exploration. Scientists and environmentalists can use VR to simulate ecological systems, examine endangered species in their habitats, and recognize the effect of weather exchange on susceptible ecosystems. By growing realistic, interactive digital environments, VR allows better information and choice-making in conservation efforts.

While VR travel and exploration provide a wealth of opportunities, there also are challenges and boundaries to bear in mind. The maximum extensive barrier is the cost of wonderful VR system, which may be out of reach for plenty customers. Additionally, the era required to create certain, immersive virtual environments can be complex and time-eating to increase, limiting the supply of positive reviews.

Moreover, VR journey is still a nascent subject, and whilst it offers exquisite potential, it can't but fully mirror the sensory reports of physical journey. The bodily sensation of motion, the capability to feel the environment, and the spontaneous interactions with others are components that VR has yet to fully seize. Despite those limitations, the potential for digital journey to supplement and beautify physical exploration is plain.

Virtual Reality has opened new frontiers in travel and exploration, permitting people to adventure to a ways-flung locations, project into area, and discover cultures and history in ways that were once impossible. Whether used for instructional functions, tourism, or expert schooling, VR is transforming the tour experience, providing new opportunities for discovery, engagement, and expertise. While demanding situations continue to be, the future of digital tour is thrilling, with the capacity to make the arena—both Earth and beyond—extra handy than ever earlier than.

CHAPTER 4

Exploring Augmented Reality

4.1. Augmented Reality Devices and Applications

Augmented Reality (AR) is a transformative era that blends the physical and digital worlds, enhancing our perception and interplay with the environment. Unlike Virtual Reality (VR), which immerses users in a completely synthetic world, AR overlays virtual information, which includes pictures, sounds, and textual content, onto the actual-global environment. This integration allows users to revel in a extra enriched reality, imparting practical programs across various industries, from entertainment to healthcare and training.

The improvement of AR technology has been carefully tied to the evolution of specialised devices that facilitate its use. These devices vary extensively in terms of shape and function, but all proportion the ability to superimpose digital content material onto the user's view of the actual international. Some of the most distinguished AR devices consist of smartphones, tablets, clever glasses, and AR headsets.

The most ubiquitous and extensively followed AR devices are smartphones and drugs. These devices use integrated cameras, sensors, and processing electricity to deliver AR reports without delay to customers' screens. Through the digital camera, smartphones capture the physical world, at the same time as the AR software overlays virtual content in real-time.

One of the important thing advantages of smartphones and tablets in AR applications is their accessibility and comfort. Almost every contemporary telephone is ready with the essential hardware and software to run AR apps, making them an less costly and effortlessly to be had option for consumers. Popular AR packages on smartphones include video games like Pokémon Go, navigation equipment along with Google Maps' AR on foot instructions, and buying apps that allow clients to visualise merchandise in their houses before purchasing.

The portability of smartphones and capsules additionally makes them best for on-the-go AR experiences. Whether navigating a city, mastering a brand new ability, or exploring a museum, these devices provide users with a bendy and interactive manner to interact with their environment.

For a extra immersive AR experience, committed clever glasses and AR headsets provide users with a fingers-free, greater integrated method of interacting with augmented content. Unlike smartphones, those gadgets are worn at once on the person's head, usually as glasses or a visor. They allow digital information to be projected into the consumer's discipline of view, leaving their arms loose to interact with the surroundings.

One of the maximum well-known AR headsets is Microsoft's HoloLens, which projects holographic photos onto the real world. The HoloLens uses advanced sensors to understand the consumer's physical surroundings, enabling it to vicinity virtual items seamlessly within the environment. This device has been specifically powerful in industrial, medical, and academic applications, where arms-unfastened, actual-time get right of entry to to information is important.

Another fantastic instance is the Magic Leap One, a pair of smart glasses designed for a extensive variety of AR programs, along with gaming, entertainment, and productiveness tools. Magic Leap's proprietary technology allows virtual content to appear as though it is a herbal part of the consumer's surroundings, growing a fairly immersive experience.

Both clever glasses and AR headsets generally consist of built-in microphones, cameras, and movement sensors, which allow for superior person interactions, which includes gesture control and voice commands. These gadgets are, but, regularly greater high-priced than smartphones and can require a higher level of technical understanding to function correctly.

The programs of AR are large and sundry, touching nearly every enterprise and revolutionizing how we interact with both the virtual and bodily worlds. Here are some key regions wherein AR is creating a big effect:

One of the most well known programs of AR is inside the retail and e-commerce industries. AR permits customers to simply attempt products earlier than making a buy, decreasing uncertainty and improving the shopping for revel in. For example, IKEA's IKEA Place app permits customers to look how fixtures would look of their homes via overlaying virtual snap shots of the products onto their physical areas via their smartphone cameras. This software helps clients visualize gadgets in their homes, ensuring that they make informed buying choices.

AR is also utilized in fashion retail, with apps like Zara and Gucci presenting virtual attempt-ons for apparel and add-ons. Consumers can see how a couple of shoes or a new jacket will look on their frame via the digicam, without having to attempt the objects on physically. This AR-more suitable buying enjoy adds comfort and interactivity to the shopping manner, specially in a international in which on line buying is increasingly famous.

In healthcare, AR is being leveraged to assist in surgical procedures, diagnostics, and patient care. AR headsets permit surgeons to overlay essential affected person statistics, along with scans and 3-D models of organs, onto the affected person's body at some stage in surgical treatment. This offers the medical professional actual-time guidance, enhancing accuracy and reducing the probability of errors. For example, AccuVein is an AR tool used to find veins for blood draws or injections, assisting medical specialists avoid unnecessary pokes or bruising.

Additionally, AR is used for clinical education and schooling. Medical college students can use AR simulations to practice strategies in a chance-free environment, gaining fingers-on revel in with complex surgeries earlier than appearing them on actual patients. This technology offers an interactive studying revel in that is a ways extra engaging and effective than traditional textbooks or 2D diagrams.

AR has extensive capability inside the discipline of training, improving mastering by way of bringing static substances to lifestyles and presenting interactive experiences. In classrooms, AR may be used to create immersive training in which college students can explore historic occasions, engage with scientific models, or visualize abstract standards in a tangible way.

For instance, AR apps like Google Expeditions permit students to take digital field journeys to places which include ancient ruins, the floor of Mars, or the human bloodstream, all from their study room. These virtual excursions convey complicated topics to lifestyles, fostering greater engagement and understanding.

In addition to classroom use, AR is likewise being applied in self-directed gaining knowledge of. Educational apps and platforms leverage AR to teach subjects starting from languages to engineering, helping users study thru immersive, palms-on experiences.

In industries like production, creation, and engineering, AR is transforming how employees perform obligations, offering real-time commands, and improving productivity. In upkeep and restore, as an example, AR applications can show step-via-step instructions and interactive diagrams that manual technicians through complex tactics, making sure that they entire obligations successfully and correctly.

For instance, Porsche makes use of AR glasses to assist technicians perform preservation on cars by displaying digital restore instructions at once in their line of sight, lowering the need for paper manuals and boosting workflow efficiency. Similarly, AR has been included into meeting strains, wherein employees can see virtual parts and tools superimposed on the actual-global assembly procedure, decreasing mistakes and dashing up production times.

The leisure enterprise has been one of the earliest and most enthusiastic adopters of AR generation, particularly in gaming. One of the first-rate-recognised examples is the mobile sport Pokémon Go, which makes use of AR to deliver virtual creatures into the actual global, encouraging gamers to discover their neighborhoods whilst interacting with these digital characters. The sport's success confirmed the sizable potential for AR in attractive users and growing interactive studies.

Additionally, AR is utilized in stay performances, inclusive of concert events and theater suggests, wherein virtual elements are superimposed onto the real-global surroundings to beautify the visual experience. For instance, artists and performers can use AR to include digital results, surroundings, or even avatars of themselves into their live indicates, creating a dynamic and immersive revel in for audiences.

The devices and packages of augmented reality are wide, and their impact on daily life keeps to develop. From smartphones to specialised headsets, AR technology is supporting us revel in the arena in new and innovative ways, remodeling industries which includes retail, healthcare, education, and amusement. As the era maintains to conform, it's miles possibly that AR turns into even greater incorporated into our every day lives, imparting greater seamless, customized, and immersive experiences that beautify our interactions with both the bodily and digital worlds.

4.2. Augmented Reality and Industry

4.2.1. Industrial Augmented Reality Applications

Augmented Reality (AR) is profoundly changing the way industries perform by merging the physical international with digital elements in real time. This fusion offers commercial sectors severa benefits, specifically in enhancing productivity, safety, and accuracy. From meeting traces to logistics, AR applications are enhancing every level of commercial workflows. Below are some of the important thing programs of AR within diverse industrial sectors.

In production, AR is used to assist workers by using overlaying virtual information onto physical components at some point of the meeting method. For example, employees on production strains can view step-through-step commands or

3D models of the products they're assembling, displayed immediately on the bodily objects. This reduces human error, complements pace, and guarantees that products are constructed efficaciously the primary time.

Companies like Siemens and Boeing are already leveraging AR of their manufacturing strategies. Siemens uses AR in its factory setups, in which employees utilize AR glasses to see instructions and real-time metrics at once on their workstations. This complements worker productiveness with the aid of disposing of the need to continuously check with paper instructions or pc displays. Similarly, Boeing uses AR in its wiring processes, wherein technicians carrying AR headsets can view wiring schematics overlaid on the aircraft, reducing the time had to deploy wiring and enhancing accuracy.

Another instance of AR in manufacturing is in first-class manipulate. With AR era, inspectors can evaluate actual-time photographs of components against 3-D models or CAD designs. Any discrepancies may be straight away recognized, reducing the time spent manually analyzing every component and growing overall best assurance.

In maintenance and repair, AR is a effective tool that offers technicians hands-loose get admission to to real-time diagnostic records and instructions whilst they may be operating on machinery or device. This allows technicians to discover problems quickly and appropriately with out the need to seek advice from manuals or troubleshoot on their personal.

Through AR, complex upkeep processes are simplified with visible aids, step-by-step steering, and even real-time remarks from experts remotely.

For example, Porsche makes use of AR in its provider facilities, presenting technicians with clever glasses that overlay protection instructions and diagrams onto the vehicle. This allows technicians carry out maintenance extra effectively and ensures that tactics are followed exactly. Similarly, AR is used in the oil and gasoline enterprise to guide employees thru protection tasks in unsafe environments, where safety is vital.

AR additionally enhances predictive renovation with the aid of allowing technicians to screen device in actual time. Sensors embedded in equipment can send information to AR gadgets, permitting employees to view the condition of gadget and assume problems earlier than they bring about failure. This predictive technique reduces downtime and improves asset toughness.

AR is likewise remodeling logistics and supply chain control by way of streamlining the procedure of tracking and dealing with inventory. In warehouses, AR applications can help employees quickly find gadgets, check inventory ranges, and get hold of actual-time updates on order statuses. Workers can use AR glasses or handheld gadgets to scan objects and automatically retrieve data on product places, decreasing the time spent looking for stock.

For example, DHL has carried out AR in its warehouses, wherein people use AR glasses to optimize the selecting process. The glasses display arrows and instructions, guiding personnel to the exact area of the product, and even advise the maximum green course to finish a mission. This no longer handiest will increase the velocity and accuracy of order success however additionally minimizes the physical strain on people, because it reduces the quantity of on foot and looking required.

In the shipping enterprise, AR is used to enhance actual-time tracking of products. By protecting digital statistics onto physical shipment, workers can right away get right of entry to statistics approximately the package deal's contents, its vacation spot, and shipping fame. This complements transparency, reduces human mistakes, and permits for faster and more efficient movement of goods.

In layout and prototyping, AR is permitting industries to visualize merchandise before they may be physically constructed. Designers can use AR to view digital prototypes of their merchandise in actual-global environments, making it simpler to spot capacity design flaws early in the development procedure. For example, automobile companies use AR to simulate how a car design will look when considered from exclusive angles and in various environments. This enables designers make modifications and enhancements in real-time, saving each time and assets.

Similarly, in the creation enterprise, AR allows architects and engineers to visualize how a building will look and feature in its real environment before production starts offevolved. They can walk round digital fashions superimposed onto production web sites, identifying capacity design issues or conflicts between special systems, along with plumbing or electric lines. This can substantially lessen the want for remodel at some point of creation, reducing fees and improving basic performance.

In the healthcare industry, AR packages have revolutionized how clinical specialists perform surgical procedures, diagnose patients, and offer care. Surgeons can use AR glasses to view crucial statistics, inclusive of MRI scans or affected person vitals, overlaid onto the patient's frame throughout surgical procedure. This allows for more particular methods and reduces the danger of mistakes.

One of the maximum outstanding packages is using AR in minimally invasive surgical procedure. Surgeons can use AR to manual gadgets via the body with more precision, improving patient results and lowering restoration times. AR is likewise used for scientific training, wherein students can exercise procedures in a managed digital surroundings earlier than running on actual sufferers.

The use of AR in commercial applications is increasing rapidly, supplying industries with the gear to enhance productiveness, safety, and general overall performance.

Whether it's improving production workflows, assisting in preservation obligations, optimizing logistics, or enabling higher layout and prototyping, AR is revolutionizing how industries operate. As the technology maintains to strengthen, its function in remodeling industries will only develop, imparting new opportunities for performance, accuracy, and innovation.

4.2.2. Augmented Reality and Education

Augmented Reality (AR) is gradually reshaping the instructional panorama by using imparting immersive and interactive getting to know reports. By merging the actual global with digital facts, AR facilitates deeper engagement and comprehension of complicated subjects. Through the use of AR era, college students are capable of engage with virtual content overlaid onto the bodily world, making learning greater dynamic and attractive. From K-12 school rooms to better education and vocational training, AR is revolutionizing training in numerous approaches.

In the traditional school room setting, AR technology serves as a effective device to beautify both teaching and getting to know. Teachers can use AR to deliver abstract ideas to life. For instance, in technological know-how training, AR can challenge 3-D fashions of molecules, anatomical structures, or maybe the sun system, allowing college students to discover these subjects in methods that static pix or diagrams on a web page can't reap. This 3-dimensional and interactive revel in now not most effective makes the learning system extra enticing however also permits for a deeper understanding of complex topics.

In history and social studies classes, AR packages can permit students to genuinely step into historic events, letting them experience and learn about history in an immersive and interactive manner. By protecting historic events and figures over their modern surroundings, AR can offer a completely unique and remarkable studying revel in that textbooks can't replicate.

For instance, packages like Google Expeditions offer virtual field journeys that permit students to discover historic ruins, well-known landmarks, or underwater environments—all without leaving the classroom. By using AR headsets or cell devices, college students can experience a virtual visit to the Great Wall of China, the Pyramids of Giza, or maybe walk on the moon, bringing instructions to lifestyles in an entirely new manner.

Augmented Reality is specifically valuable in vocational and technical schooling, where arms-on studying is crucial. In fields consisting of medicine, engineering, and professional trades, AR is getting used to simulate actual-international scenarios for students to exercise with out the hazard of mistakes or harm to equipment. In medical training, AR allows students to explore human anatomy in 3 dimensions and behavior virtual surgical procedures, offering a secure and managed environment for learning complicated strategies.

For instance, AR apps can project a holographic photo of a human body onto a flat floor, permitting college students to engage with and manage the organs, bones, and muscles as though they had been physically present. This method of gaining knowledge of permits college students to visualize the shape and function of human anatomy in a way that static textbooks or -dimensional pix can not achieve. Similarly, in fields like engineering, AR permits students to visualize 3-D fashions of machinery and systems, enabling them to better recognize how components suit collectively and function.

In technical trades consisting of electric work or automobile restore, AR structures can manual college students thru complicated tactics, offering actual-time, step-via-step commands which might be overlaid onto the real machinery. This enhances the learning enjoy via allowing students to carry out responsibilities with the support of visible prompts and without the want for big trainer intervention.

One of the maximum considerable advantages of AR in education is its capability to create customized studying reports. Students have special learning patterns and paces, and AR lets in for adaptive, custom designed gaining knowledge of pathways. With AR technology, college students can interact with mastering substances at their very own tempo, revisiting standards that they find challenging or progressing thru fabric that they draw close quick. This level of personalization facilitates to make sure that each pupil gets the support they want to prevail.

For example, AR equipment may be designed to evolve in real-time to a scholar's development, providing extra help or demanding situations based totally on their performance. In language getting to know, AR packages can use voice recognition and contextual clues to assist students practice pronunciation, grammar, and vocabulary in actual-world conditions. Similarly, AR can support unique training by way of imparting multisensory getting to know stories that have interaction students with various gaining knowledge of needs, supporting them higher recognize principles and interact with their environment.

AR fosters collaboration via enabling college students to have interaction with each virtual and physical factors in actual-time. This interactivity makes AR a powerful tool for organization studying, permitting students to paintings collectively on tasks or experiments that integrate the real international with virtual overlays. Collaborative AR reviews can be mainly useful in STEM schooling, in which students can paintings collectively to resolve complicated troubles or behavior experiments that they would now not be capable of carry out in my view.

For instance, in an engineering elegance, college students could paintings in organizations to collect and test a digital prototype. AR can assignment the 3-D model of the prototype into their environment, permitting them to manage, analyze, and check the version collaboratively. This fingers-on technique enables college students expand teamwork, problem-solving, and essential questioning talents even as also reinforcing the technical expertise they need for his or her discipline.

Moreover, AR promotes energetic gaining knowledge of with the aid of imparting instant comments. As college students interact with AR content material, they are able to acquire real-time exams and suggestions for development, encouraging deeper engagement with the fabric and fostering a greater lively, participatory studying environment.

AR is also making training more available with the aid of overcoming geographical and physical obstacles. With the rise of far flung mastering and online education, AR generation permits students to have interaction with academic content material in a extra immersive manner, although they're positioned far from traditional gaining knowledge of establishments. Students can use AR apps to get admission to virtual school rooms, engage with peers, and take part in academic sports, all from the comfort in their homes.

In areas where get entry to to first-rate training is confined because of geographical or socio-financial factors, AR offers an revolutionary answer. By offering cheap and on hand getting to know reports, AR can help bridge the education gap and offer college students in far off areas with opportunities to study and interact with content that would otherwise be unavailable to them.

The destiny of AR in education holds even extra capacity. As AR generation will become more superior, more academic content and equipment can be advanced, imparting richer, extra attractive getting to know studies. In the future, we are able to anticipate even extra sizable adoption of AR in school rooms, with interactive textbooks, digital lab experiments, and immersive simulations becoming the norm. The opportunities for integrating AR into training are big, presenting new approaches for college kids to examine, collaborate, and enjoy the arena.

With advancements in AR hardware, along with extra less expensive and effective AR glasses, and enhancements in content material shipping systems, AR will keep to extend its role in schooling, supplying college students of all ages and backgrounds the potential to engage with their studying in new and innovative approaches. As the technology matures, its capability to adapt to the wishes of numerous learners will make certain that AR will become an crucial a part of the schooling gadget in the future years.

AR is remodeling schooling by making mastering more engaging, personalized, and interactive. It breaks down the traditional barriers of the classroom and allows college students to revel in education in totally new ways. With its capability to beautify expertise, foster collaboration, and offer immersive mastering stories, AR is set to play a important function in shaping the destiny of schooling.

4.3. Augmented Reality inside the Business World

Augmented Reality (AR) has emerged as a transformative technology inside the enterprise global, reshaping industries across the globe. By covering digital content onto the real international, AR creates immersive studies that decorate client interactions, improve operational efficiencies, and streamline product development. Businesses, from retail to manufacturing, healthcare to real estate, are embracing AR for its ability to foster innovation, optimize techniques, and deliver precise reviews.

One of the maximum distinguished uses of AR in enterprise is in improving client reviews. Retailers, as an example, are the use of AR to create interactive buying environments that blend the virtual with the bodily. By integrating AR into their stores and cell apps, organizations permit clients to interact with merchandise in methods that had been previously not possible. In style, for instance, AR enables shoppers to clearly try on garments or add-ons, supporting them visualize how a product will look earlier than making a buy. Similarly, domestic fixtures organizations provide AR answers that permit clients visualize how a piece of furnishings will look of their residing rooms via simply using their smartphones or pills.

The automobile enterprise has additionally seen AR adoption to improve the patron revel in. Car manufacturers are integrating AR in showrooms, allowing customers to interact with 3D models of cars, change shades or configurations, or even test power vehicles in a simulated environment. This not simplest offers a more engaging way for clients to discover vehicles but additionally reduces the need for physical stock, saving on showroom area and sources.

By providing personalised, immersive studies, AR enables businesses to interact purchasers extra deeply and creates a feel of pleasure and convenience that conventional shopping strategies can not reflect. The potential to peer how a product will look or perform in a real-international placing earlier than purchase can cause better customer pleasure and greater sales conversion quotes.

AR era is being more and more used to optimize operations and enhance workforce efficiency in numerous industries. In production, AR permits employees to get entry to real-time records, instructions, and steerage even as appearing tasks, assisting to lessen mistakes and improve productivity. For example, AR can show step-through-step meeting instructions for technicians immediately of their line of sight, reducing the need for paper manuals or in search of help from supervisors. This is especially useful in industries along with aerospace and automotive production, in which precision and efficiency are vital.

In warehouses and logistics, AR is also revolutionizing stock management. By using AR glasses or cell gadgets, warehouse people can get right of entry to stay stock facts and get hold of actual-time instructions on wherein to find items, improving order picking efficiency. Additionally, AR can offer people with real-time updates on the location of goods, decreasing the time spent trying to find items and minimizing errors so as success.

Another location where AR is enhancing business operations is inside the discipline of renovation and repairs. Technicians can use AR devices to overlay real-time data, schematics, or diagnostic records onto equipment, assisting them to troubleshoot issues extra effectively. This era reduces downtime and complements the speed and accuracy of maintenance, in the long run improving the lowest line via preserving operations strolling smoothly.

AR is likewise reworking product layout and development by way of offering designers, engineers, and product builders with a greater interactive and green manner to visualise prototypes and ideas. Rather than depending solely on physical fashions or drawings, designers can use AR to project 3D models into the real world and manage them in real-time. This permits for quicker new release and testing of product ideas, enabling businesses to lessen development instances and enhance the overall pleasant in their products.

In industries like architecture and creation, AR is being used to visualize homes, systems, and indoors designs earlier than creation starts offevolved. Architects can overlay 3-d fashions of homes on-web page, supplying stakeholders with a clear expertise of the proposed layout and helping to pick out any ability issues early inside the manner. This now not best saves time and money with the aid of lowering highly-priced design revisions however also helps better collaboration between designers, engineers, and clients.

Similarly, AR is revolutionizing the prototyping manner in industries inclusive of purchaser electronics and car. Engineers can visualize and check new components or gadgets in a real-international context the use of AR, making adjustments based totally on how the design interacts with its environment. This type of immersive prototyping streamlines product development and enables faster innovation cycles.

AR is likewise a powerful marketing device, permitting corporations to create memorable, interactive campaigns that engage customers in new methods. Marketers are the usage of AR to create campaigns that inspire clients to engage with products or commercials in a extra dynamic and attractive way. For instance, AR lets in organizations to convert traditional print advertisements into interactive experiences, wherein clients can experiment a mag advert or a billboard to liberate extra content, including motion pictures, product demos, or special offers.

In the enjoyment enterprise, AR is being used to create interactive studies that immerse clients in branded content. For example, some corporations have launched AR-powered games or apps that integrate their products or services, encouraging purchasers to interact with the emblem in an exciting and noteworthy way. This form of engagement strengthens emblem loyalty and facilitates corporations stand out in a crowded marketplace.

AR can also be used in live occasions and exhibitions, supplying attendees interactive, immersive reviews. For example, change display cubicles can combine AR to permit ability clients to visualise products in 3-D or maybe interact with digital variations of the product. This can make product demonstrations greater enticing and informative, ultimately increasing consumer hobby and sales.

In addition to enhancing client stories and operational efficiencies, AR is likewise transforming the manner businesses method schooling and remote collaboration. For industries with complicated gadget or procedures, AR can offer immersive education packages that simulate actual-world scenarios, permitting personnel to practice their abilties in a controlled surroundings. This is especially beneficial in sectors like healthcare, aviation, and heavy industry, where arms-on enjoy is important for making sure protection and effectiveness.

AR is also getting used to facilitate far flung collaboration between groups spread across distinctive places. Through AR, groups can interact with digital models, proportion information, and talk in real-time, enhancing productivity and trouble-fixing. For example, engineers running on a complicated undertaking can collaborate in reality by using interacting with 3-D fashions or blueprints overlaid onto their physical environment, enabling them to work together as if they had been in the same room.

Remote training can also be drastically more advantageous with AR. Instead of relying on conventional video tutorials or static documentation, employees can have interaction in immersive training classes, receiving real-time feedback and guidance. This no longer handiest makes training extra effective however additionally reduces the need for in-individual sessions, saving time and assets.

As AR generation continues to conform, its programs in enterprise are predicted to grow even in addition. With advancements in hardware, consisting of more powerful AR glasses and stepped forward mobile gadgets, corporations may have get admission to to even greater sophisticated AR tools to improve operations, layout, advertising and marketing, and customer support.

In the near future, we can expect to look extra vast adoption of AR throughout industries, with corporations of all sizes leveraging the generation to improve efficiency, beautify client reports, and power innovation. The potential for AR to convert enterprise operations, advertising techniques, and product improvement is great, and its growing integration into normal enterprise practices promises to make it an essential tool for the contemporary business enterprise.

Augmented Reality isn't only a futuristic technology; it's far already creating a enormous effect on agencies today. By imparting improved purchaser reports, improving operational efficiencies, revolutionizing product layout, and remodeling advertising strategies, AR is supporting businesses live competitive in an increasingly more virtual international. As the era matures, its capability for driving business innovation will hold to expand, similarly embedding AR into the material of current commercial enterprise practices.

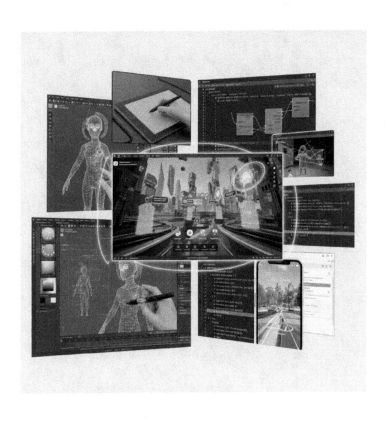

CHAPTER 5

Content Creation in Virtual Reality and Augmented Reality

5.1. 3-D Modeling and Design

The creation of 3-D content material performs a fundamental position within the development of each Virtual Reality (VR) and Augmented Reality (AR) stories. From gaming and amusement to business applications and educational equipment, 3D models function the spine of interactive, immersive environments that users engage with in digital and augmented areas.

5.1.1. 3-D Modeling and Design Techniques

3-D modeling is the method of creating a mathematical representation of a 3-dimensional object or surface the use of specialised software. These fashions can range from simple objects to tremendously detailed, complex systems, and they're essential in growing digital worlds, simulations, and experiences in both VR and AR environments. The process of 3-D modeling involves several key techniques, which include mesh modeling, sculpting, procedural modeling, and texture mapping.

Mesh modeling is the maximum common method utilized in 3-D design. It involves the creation of gadgets by defining a network of vertices, edges, and faces that shape the model's structure, referred to as a "mesh." These factors are linked to form the fundamental form of an object. Mesh modeling is widely utilized in VR and AR due to the fact it's far noticeably flexible and permits for the introduction of exact and correct models of items, environments, and characters.

This technique requires the designer to carefully plan the topology of the model to make certain that it deforms effectively whilst animated and is rendered successfully in real-time applications. For example, while modeling a individual for a VR recreation or AR software, the version's mesh needs to be optimized to ensure it may be rendered smoothly on quite a few devices, from excessive-stop VR headsets to cellular phones.

Sculpting is a more organic modeling technique that intently mimics conventional clay sculpting. In this technique, designers manage a 3-d floor as if it have been a physical fabric, the use of gear that push, pull, and smooth the surface. Sculpting is regularly used to create tremendously exact models, which include characters, creatures, and complicated systems, that require elaborate information and clean, fluid surfaces.

One of the advantages of sculpting is that it allows for a extra intuitive, inventive method to 3-d design, which is specially beneficial when creating organic shapes or textures that could be tough to gain with mesh modeling. In VR and AR improvement, sculpting is specially valuable for growing lifelike characters or exact environments that need to look sensible and immersive when customers have interaction with them in a virtual space.

Procedural modeling includes the usage of algorithms and mathematical features to automatically generate 3D objects or environments based totally on predefined regulations. This technique is specifically beneficial in developing big-scale environments including landscapes, cityscapes, or other widespread scenes. Instead of manually modeling each tree or building, procedural modeling allows developers to generate massive, complex worlds fast and successfully.

In VR and AR programs, procedural modeling can be specially useful for developing expansive worlds that customers can discover, inclusive of open-global games or simulations. By the use of procedural era techniques, builders can create an ever-increasing, dynamic virtual surroundings that feels big and interactive, without having to manually layout every unmarried object in the international.

Once the 3D model's geometry is created, the subsequent step within the system is texture mapping. This includes applying textures to the version's surface to provide it colour, detail, and realism. Textures may be anything from easy styles to complex pix that simulate materials like wood, metallic, or skin. Shading refers to the manner mild interacts with the version's floor to create outcomes like shadows, reflections, and highlights.

In VR and AR content, the great of texture mapping and shading is crucial for developing visually practical stories. For instance, in a VR sport, the textures and shading of a man or woman's garments or an surroundings's walls can make the difference among an immersive experience and one which feels flat or synthetic. Designers use diverse mapping strategies, along with bump mapping, ordinary mapping, and displacement mapping, to provide surfaces realistic intensity and detail, that is critical in VR and AR packages wherein realism and immersion are key to the person revel in.

For interactive and dynamic content, 3-D fashions often want to be rigged and lively. Rigging is the system of including a skeleton to a 3-D version so it is able to pass in a realistic manner. This is especially crucial for characters or items that want to be lively, including in VR video games or education simulations. Once the rigging is whole, animators can upload movement by defining the person's or object's variety of movement and how it behaves in one-of-a-kind scenarios.

Animation strategies like keyframing, movement capture, and procedural animation are often utilized in VR and AR content advent. These methods help carry 3-D models to lifestyles via making them flow, have interaction, and reply to the surroundings, ensuring that users have a continuing, enticing enjoy in virtual or augmented environments.

For VR and AR, it's miles crucial that 3-D models are optimized for real-time rendering, meaning they can be rendered effectively and easily as the consumer interacts with the virtual environment. Optimization includes reducing the complexity of the version whilst preserving its appearance and functionality. Techniques along with polygon discount, texture compression, and LOD (Level of Detail) are generally hired to make sure that 3-D models run smoothly on a whole lot of hardware platforms, from high-quit gaming PCs and VR headsets to cell AR applications.

In VR, performance is specially critical because a lag or stutter in the rendering of a 3-d model can destroy the immersive experience and lead to motion sickness or consumer pain. Thus, growing fashions that balance detail with efficiency is a key consideration in VR and AR layout.

The techniques mentioned above are vital for developing compelling, interactive, and visually attractive VR and AR experiences. Whether growing a virtual global for gaming, an educational tool for training, or an augmented truth app for shopping, the achievement of these studies relies upon on the fine of the 3-D fashions and their integration into the general design.

In VR, 3-d modeling lets in for the introduction of entirely immersive environments that customers can interact with, ranging from sensible simulations to fantastical worlds. Similarly, in AR, 3-D models are overlaid onto the actual international, enabling customers to engage with digital objects as though they have been a part of their physical environment. As VR and AR technologies keep to adapt, the call for for more sophisticated 3D modeling strategies will best develop, pushing the boundaries of what is possible in growing virtual and augmented experiences.

3-d modeling and layout are foundational factors of VR and AR content material creation, driving the development of immersive, interactive, and visually stunning experiences. From the preliminary design of basic items to the creation of fairly specific characters and environments, those strategies are essential to constructing attractive digital worlds and enhancing the consumer revel in. As VR and AR maintain to boost, the strategies and gear utilized in 3-d modeling will evolve, enabling even extra realistic, dynamic, and interactive content material.

5.1.2. Detailed Modeling of Digital Twins

Digital twins constitute digital replicas of bodily objects, systems, or procedures, serving as dynamic simulations that reflect their actual-international opposite numbers in real-time. This distinctive modeling method is important for developing correct, dependable, and interactive digital twins that may be used throughout various industries, such as production, healthcare, city planning, and extra. The essence of digital dual modeling is to capture the complexities of real-global gadgets and systems, permitting better evaluation, monitoring, and choice-making.

The first step in distinctive modeling is accumulating records from the bodily device a good way to be reflected within the virtual dual. This records generally includes a mixture of sensor information, operational records, and historical performance records, all of which offer the inspiration for growing an correct digital reproduction.

In many cases, sensors embedded in bodily objects or structures (together with machines, buildings, or maybe complete towns) continuously display a huge range of parameters, including temperature, stress, humidity, velocity, and position. This real-time facts is vital in ensuring that the digital twin appropriately represents the modern-day state of the physical counterpart.

Moreover, for greater complex systems, historic information is regularly used to model tendencies and behaviors through the years, which helps in predicting destiny performance and identifying capacity failures or inefficiencies. This data may be amassed through Internet of Things (IoT) gadgets, gadget mastering models, or maybe manual records access, depending on the character of the machine being modeled.

Once the actual-global data is accrued, the subsequent step is to create the virtual version on the way to mirror the physical gadget. This involves the use of specialized software program equipment that allow for the creation of 3-d models, CAD (Computer-Aided Design) drawings, and simulations.

For example, in manufacturing, distinct digital twins of machinery or manufacturing strains are created the usage of CAD software program. These fashions have to capture each issue of the system, right down to the smallest detail, to mirror the bodily environment as it should be. The digital model may additionally include specs like material sorts, factor geometries, weight distributions, and movement constraints, all of that are derived from the statistics accrued.

Moreover, if the gadget being modeled includes mechanical or electrical additives, it's miles vital to consist of the technical elements, along with the interactions between distinct parts, in addition to operational parameters like strength intake, warmth generation, or fluid dynamics. The more particular and precise the model, the more as it should be it can mirror actual-international behavior.

A key function of virtual twins is their capacity to update in actual time based totally on statistics from their bodily opposite numbers. To reap this, the digital model need to be incorporated with actual-time records resources, permitting it to mirror the contemporary state of the physical device at any given second. This requires sophisticated information integration methods that can deal with massive volumes of continuous data even as making sure the accuracy and responsiveness of the virtual dual.

For example, within the case of clever towns, virtual twins are regularly connected to numerous sensors embedded in the course of the metropolis infrastructure, together with visitors lights, water deliver systems, and energy grids. By constantly feeding the virtual version with information from these sensors, the virtual twin can update in actual-time, providing a live simulation of town operations. This allows metropolis planners and engineers to screen systems, become aware of inefficiencies, and make knowledgeable decisions on the fly.

Similarly, inside the car enterprise, virtual twins of motors are built to simulate the performance of different additives, including the engine, brakes, and suspension gadget, under diverse situations. These simulations can then be adjusted in actual-time as information from the automobile's sensors is integrated, bearing in mind predictive preservation, optimization, and actual-time troubleshooting.

Detailed modeling of virtual twins extends past actual-time records integration and consists of superior simulations and predictive modeling techniques. The goal right here is to now not most effective reflect the bodily device but also predict destiny behaviors and become aware of capability issues earlier than they occur.

For instance, in industrial packages, virtual twins can simulate put on and tear on machines, predicting whilst a thing is in all likelihood to fail primarily based on elements along with usage patterns, operating situations, and environmental variables. This predictive maintenance capability is one of the most valuable factors of virtual twins, as it allows for timely interventions that may reduce downtime and save you expensive maintenance.

Similarly, virtual twins inside the healthcare industry are used to simulate the behavior of medical devices or even whole organ structures in the human frame. By analyzing a affected person's real-time records along the virtual dual, healthcare specialists can are expecting how positive remedies or interventions will affect the affected person's situation, optimizing care and enhancing consequences.

One of the challenges in special modeling of virtual twins is making sure scalability and flexibility. As systems develop in complexity, the digital twin must be able to scale for this reason, regularly incorporating additional statistics resources, components, or operational capabilities.

In some cases, virtual twins want to version systems that aren't static however evolve over time. For example, inside the creation industry, digital twins are used to song the development of a building's construction, updating as new substances are introduced, and the structure takes shape. These fashions need to accommodate consistent adjustments while nonetheless retaining accuracy and overall performance.

Moreover, as virtual twin technology advances, there is growing call for for adaptability, wherein models may be customized for one-of-a-kind packages. The identical virtual twin of a chunk of machinery, for instance, can be utilized in numerous contexts, together with predictive renovation, performance evaluation, or lifecycle control, and should be flexible enough to serve every of these purposes successfully.

Creating a detailed virtual dual regularly involves collaboration across more than one teams and stakeholders. Engineers, facts scientists, designers, and area specialists have to work together to ensure that the digital dual appropriately displays the complexities of the physical device. Moreover, the combination of facts from various assets – from sensors to IoT networks to legacy databases – calls for sturdy collaboration between IT departments, business leaders, and technical teams.

Furthermore, in huge-scale programs, together with digital twins utilized in smart cities or commercial techniques, a couple of digital twins may additionally want to be related or integrated into a unified system. This allows for a complete assessment of complicated structures, enabling better decision-making and aid allocation.

Detailed modeling of virtual twins is a extraordinarily complex but crucial system for developing accurate, interactive, and scalable digital representations of bodily systems. By integrating actual-time records, making use of advanced simulation techniques, and ensuring adaptability, virtual twins provide precious insights into how systems behave, expect capacity problems, and optimize overall performance. As digital twin technology keeps to adapt, the precision and talents of these fashions will extend, allowing deeper integration with actual-world operations and fostering extra efficient and sustainable practices across industries.

5.2. Content Creation and Programming

Content introduction and programming are critical components of developing immersive stories in both virtual fact (VR) and augmented reality (AR). These methods contain designing, coding, and enforcing the interactive elements that force the engagement and functionality of digital worlds. While the intention is to create reports which might be visually stunning and noticeably purposeful, the underlying work calls for a deep understanding of both innovative and technical components.

The first step in content material creation for VR and AR is designing interactive digital environments that experience intuitive and tasty. In virtual reality, the environment is totally artificial, and the person interacts with it as although it had been real. For augmented truth, the design consists of masking digital factors onto actual-global environments, requiring cautious attention to how those elements blend seamlessly with bodily environment.

Designing these environments includes operating with specialised 3-d modeling tools and software. Tools like Blender, Autodesk Maya, or Unity are broadly used to create 3-D objects, textures, and environments. These digital creations are then incorporated into the VR or AR platform to create a cohesive revel in. The goal is to ensure that the environment feels natural to the consumer, whether or not they are exploring a futuristic metropolis in VR or interacting with a digital overlay in the real global via AR.

To enhance the experience of immersion, designers ought to don't forget spatial interactions, intensity, and scale. In VR, it's far crucial to make certain that objects seem life like and that movement thru the environment feels realistic. In AR, the venture is to make sure that digital items in shape obviously inside the user's bodily environment, adjusting in actual-time to adjustments in lights, angle, and motion.

Programming is the backbone of creating VR and AR environments interactive. It is thru programming that the digital elements inside those environments reply to person moves, creating engaging and dynamic reports.

For VR, programming commonly entails writing code that permits users to engage with objects using movement controllers, haptic remarks gadgets, or maybe their very own hand moves, depending on the level of immersion preferred. This calls for the integration of hardware (consisting of VR headsets and controllers) with software. The maximum generally used structures for VR content material advent are Unity and Unreal Engine, each of which provide the equipment necessary for developing immersive interactive studies. These engines assist languages like C# (Unity) or C (Unreal Engine), allowing developers to create interactive structures that react to person enter.

In augmented reality, programming additionally plays a considerable position in item placement, tracking, and interplay. AR improvement frameworks, inclusive of ARKit for iOS and ARCore for Android, provide sturdy toolsets for integrating AR factors with the actual international. Through these frameworks, developers can write code that tracks the user's surroundings and position, permitting virtual gadgets to seem anchored in actual-world places. For instance, whilst a person points their phone at a road corner, AR may display a digital shop, complete with interactive features like virtual buttons or maps. The interplay among digital gadgets and the physical global requires specific programming to make sure that digital content material responds accurately to the consumer's actions, vicinity, and environmental modifications.

One of the important thing elements in content material creation and programming for VR and AR is the mixing of real-time data. This is especially critical for programs like virtual twins or live records visualization in AR. For example, in a virtual fact setting designed for medical training, real-time facts from patient monitoring device may be integrated to simulate real-lifestyles situations. In AR, actual-time statistics is probably used to superimpose crucial records over a patient's frame in the course of surgical treatment or display live visitors data overlaid on a map.

The integration of actual-time facts into a VR or AR revel in regularly calls for advanced programming capabilities, as builders ought to create systems which can manage massive streams of statistics without compromising the overall performance of the environment. To ensure clean and responsive stories, builders have to use green algorithms, optimize information glide, and manage sources correctly. Moreover, APIs (Application Programming Interfaces) are often used to connect outside records resources with the VR or AR revel in, permitting actual-time updates to be contemplated inside the digital global.

In VR and AR, programming isn't always just about creating static environments; it's also about developing interactive elements that permit users to interact with the virtual global. This includes scripting behaviors inclusive of object manipulation, animations, and triggering occasions primarily based on user input. These interactions are critical for growing experiences that experience alive and responsive.

In VR, interplay can take the shape of bodily gestures, item grabs, or button presses on controllers. For instance, a VR game may require gamers to choose up items, remedy puzzles, or navigate environments the usage of hand gestures or controller inputs. The programming concerned in those movements needs to account for a wide sort of consumer interactions, including button mapping, collision detection, and remarks loops (together with haptic vibration while an object is picked up). The programming must ensure that those interactions feel herbal, seamless, and responsive.

Similarly, in AR, interactivity is crucial to the enjoy. AR packages regularly permit customers to control digital gadgets in real-global environments. For instance, an AR app would possibly allow customers to drag and scale digital furniture to suit a room's layout. This calls for complicated tracking algorithms and specific calibration to make sure that digital gadgets flow easily inside the real international, maintaining proper spatial relationships and scale. Additionally, AR packages might need to recognize and reply to bodily surfaces, lighting fixtures situations, or even consumer gestures, all of which require superior programming abilties.

An regularly-unnoticed however crucial aspect of VR and AR content material introduction is optimization. Given the immersive and interactive nature of those technology, clean overall performance is crucial to prevent discomfort and make sure person delight. VR and AR content material should run at high body costs (generally 60 frames in line with 2d or better) to keep away from troubles like movement illness or lag.

Optimizing VR and AR content material involves decreasing the computational load with out sacrificing visual excellent. This may also consist of optimizing 3D models, decreasing polygon counts, compressing textures, and the use of green shaders to decorate overall performance. Additionally, developers need to ensure that the applications are optimized for one-of-a-kind platforms, whether or not they are standalone VR headsets, smartphones, or high-stop PCs.

In AR, optimization may be mainly tough because of the need to music real-world environments in real time at the same time as rendering virtual gadgets as it should be. As users flow thru a physical area, the AR machine have to continuously replace its knowledge of the surroundings, which may be computationally intensive. To deal with this, builders rent techniques together with SLAM (Simultaneous Localization and Mapping) to song the person's position while keeping premiere performance.

Creating immersive VR and AR reviews is often a collaborative technique that brings together plenty of specialists, which includes designers, programmers, sound engineers, and 3-D artists. These groups paintings together to make certain that the content material is visually attractive, functionally sound, and interactive.

Creative teams attention at the creative aspects of VR and AR content, designing environments, characters, and items which can be visually engaging. Technical groups, however, handle the programming, optimization, and performance factors of the revel in. Effective communique and collaboration among these two groups are important for generating high-quality content.

In huge-scale VR and AR projects, which include simulations for industries like aerospace or healthcare, the mixing of domain-particular understanding is likewise vital. Engineers, clinical experts, and enterprise specialists contribute their information to make certain that the digital content material as it should be reflects actual-global techniques, presenting sensible and effective schooling or analysis equipment.

Content advent and programming for virtual reality and augmented truth are foundational to delivering immersive, interactive reviews. From designing and modeling digital worlds to coding interactions and integrating real-time information, every step requires a deep expertise of each innovative layout and technical knowledge. As VR and AR technology retain to conform, the equipment and strategies for creating content turns into greater superior, allowing even more dynamic and attractive studies. By getting to know content material creation and programming, builders can push the bounds of virtual and augmented environments, supplying customers genuinely transformative stories.

5.3. Creating Interactive Virtual Worlds

Creating interactive digital worlds is at the heart of immersive reviews in digital reality (VR) and augmented fact (AR). These digital environments aren't merely passive spaces; they're designed to react to and have interaction the consumer, making them an integral part of the experience. The aim is to foster a feel of presence and interplay, making sure customers experience as although they're honestly a part of the surroundings.

5.3.1. Principles of Designing Interactive Virtual Worlds

The manner of designing interactive digital worlds entails a mix of artistic imaginative and prescient, technical information, and person-focused layout. Several key principles manual the creation of those immersive spaces, helping make sure they may be enticing, intuitive, and interactive.

The basis of any interactive digital world is the experience of immersion, which is the feeling of being found in a virtual area. Immersion is completed through sensory input, consisting of visible, auditory, and every now and then haptic feedback. In VR, visual immersion is in most cases executed by using creating tremendous 3-D environments with practical textures, lighting, and physics. However, it's now not pretty much creating reasonable environments; immersion also is predicated on how properly the environment responds to person moves. This sense of presence is critical because it makes the person feel that they are truly "inside" the world they may be experiencing.

In augmented truth, immersion takes on a barely exclusive meaning. The real international stays vital, but digital factors are overlaid and integrated seamlessly into the physical surroundings. To acquire immersion in AR, designers ought to make certain that digital objects engage in plausible ways with the actual world, appearing to physically occupy real area in preference to floating unnaturally.

One of the core tenets of interactive digital worlds is the potential to interact the consumer actively. This interactivity can take many paperwork, from manipulating objects inside the environment to solving puzzles, navigating complicated areas, or maybe interacting with digital characters. The aim is to make the user experience like their actions have an effect on the arena around them.

For VR, interactivity generally includes the use of controllers, hand-tracking, or different types of enter to permit the user to govern items, flow thru the environment, or cause occasions. VR environments are designed in order that the person's actions within the digital area without delay affect the simulation. For instance, a consumer might choose up a digital object and have a look at it from extraordinary angles, or they is probably required to have interaction with various components of the surroundings to remedy demanding situations or development in a narrative.

In AR, interactivity often consists of moves like tapping on digital gadgets or manipulating them in real time. AR systems need to be capable of track the user's function inside the physical international to make sure that virtual gadgets appear to live in vicinity or engage with actual-world environment in a herbal way. For example, an AR app would possibly permit users to pull and drop virtual furnishings right into a actual room, adjusting the placement based totally at the person's viewpoint.

Effective navigation inside a virtual global is crucial to creating an interactive revel in. The user have to be able to flow thru the surroundings in a manner that feels natural and intuitive. This is specially crucial in VR, where customers can pass in any direction, doubtlessly making them feel disoriented if the surroundings isn't always designed with right spatial cognizance in mind.

To hold spatial awareness, VR worlds are frequently designed with landmarks or navigational aids to guide the user. This may want to consist of an on-display screen map, visual cues, or haptic comments that allows the user orient themselves. Additionally, VR environments often hire easy locomotion techniques, which include teleportation, to mitigate motion sickness and allow for snug movement throughout big virtual areas.

In AR, spatial cognizance is simply as critical, but the user's navigation is within a physical area. AR systems frequently want to apprehend environmental functions, inclusive of walls or tables, and adjust the site of digital elements hence. For instance, when placing digital objects in an AR enjoy, the device need to make certain that the objects take a seat successfully on surfaces, reply to the user's moves, and behave in ways that make sense inside the real-global context.

A properly-designed interactive virtual international should be reachable to all users, no matter their enjoy with VR/AR technology. This calls for knowledge the desires and alternatives of various customers, such as those with disabilities. For example, VR stories have to be designed to keep away from inflicting discomfort, which includes motion illness or eye stress, whilst still offering an interesting environment.

In phrases of interactivity, consumer-centered design means ensuring that the controls and interactions are intuitive and responsive. For VR, this entails designing controller schemes or hand gestures which can be smooth to research and use. For AR, it'd include making sure that the digital objects can be manipulated thru simple gestures or voice instructions, ensuring that users of varying competencies can interact with the content.

Moreover, user-centered design additionally entails crafting stories that healthy the cognitive and emotional needs of the customers. This method growing environments that offer a stability of mission and praise, with intuitive interfaces that encourage exploration and discovery. For example, a VR game need to provide interactive elements which are rewarding however not frustrating, preserving the person's engagement over the years.

Real-time comments is important for keeping customers engaged in an interactive digital international. This remarks can take various forms, consisting of visual modifications, auditory cues, or haptic responses, all of which tell the consumer approximately the impact of their actions on the virtual surroundings.

In VR, feedback mechanisms should involve visible indicators, including a color change whilst an object is picked up, or auditory comments, like a sound impact while the user triggers an movement. Haptic remarks, like vibration in a controller, can simulate the sensation of interacting with objects, including a tactile measurement to the virtual experience. This instant remarks loop reinforces the experience that the person's moves are significant within the digital international.

For AR, actual-time comments can be further dynamic. For example, as a person moves their device around a room, an AR app might modify the position of virtual furniture in real time, presenting remarks on how nicely the digital gadgets align with physical surroundings. This sort of interplay encourages users to experiment and discover, as their movements cause instant and observable changes inside the surroundings.

Narrative performs a critical role in many interactive digital worlds. Well-designed storytelling can flip a easy virtual environment right into a compelling enjoy. In VR and AR, storytelling frequently takes the shape of branching narratives, interactive characters, or environmental storytelling, in which the world itself conveys a tale through visual cues, artifacts, and world-building.

Interactive narratives in VR can be immersive and enormously personalized, with users making choices that affect the development of the story. For instance, in VR function-playing video games, gamers can also interact with characters or resolve troubles that have an effect on the final results of the sport. In AR, storytelling can be less linear however can nevertheless contain guiding customers through narratives that spread as they interact with their bodily environment.

Creating interactive virtual worlds calls for a balance among design, programming, and person enjoy. By adhering to standards like immersion, interactivity, spatial cognizance, and consumer-targeted layout, developers can create environments that aren't handiest enticing but also intuitive and handy. As era continues to adapt, so too will the methods wherein we layout and interact with digital worlds, pushing the bounds of what is feasible in each digital fact and augmented fact.

5.3.2. Tips for Enhancing User Experience

Creating a compelling consumer experience in virtual fact (VR) and augmented fact (AR) requires more than just technical proficiency. It entails addressing both the emotional and sensible elements of interaction, ensuring the environment is enticing, immersive, and intuitive. The purpose is to make the user experience connected to the digital world in a manner that feels natural and exciting.

One of the important thing factors in enhancing user revel in is making sure seamless interplay. The much less substantial the technology, the extra immersive the enjoy becomes. Delays, glitches, or awkward controls can disrupt the go with the flow of the revel in and damage the experience of presence. To obtain this, builders ought to recognition on minimizing latency, which can be especially elaborate in VR. High latency leads to a postpone among the person's moves and the device's response, that could purpose pain, mainly in fast-shifting environments. Reducing this latency guarantees smoother, more natural interactions. Additionally, intuitive manage schemes are critical. Whether it entails the use of hand controllers, gestures, or gaze monitoring, the consumer interface need to experience natural and simple. For VR, this might mean replicating actual-international moves as carefully as possible, and for AR, gesture-based controls or voice commands must be responsive and without difficulty comprehensible.

Immersive comments plays an equally critical function. When users have interaction with the virtual world, they must get hold of instant and clean feedback to boost the feel of involvement. This remarks can are available many paperwork, which include visible cues which includes shade changes, auditory indicators like sounds or song, or haptic feedback through vibrations in the controller. These signals offer a response to the person's actions, solidifying their connection to the virtual surroundings.

Another fundamental attention is ensuring comfort, as VR and AR can sometimes cause discomfort or maybe movement illness. In VR, issues like motion sickness can arise while the virtual movements are not aligned with the person's bodily moves. This is especially common while there may be a put off among what the consumer expects to manifest and what the machine provides. To deal with this, builders can offer options to regulate movement speeds or introduce extra sluggish transitions among states. It also allows to layout constant points inside the digital surroundings—visible landmarks or interactive gadgets that help users orient themselves. Fixed points act as anchors, offering users with a experience of course and stability as they navigate the gap.

In addition to comfort, creating attractive and interactive content is crucial to maintaining consumer interest. A digital international or revel in can most effective be immersive if it captures the user's attention and holds it. This is wherein gamification may be a powerful tool. Introducing recreation-like elements which include scoring structures, achievements, or challenges can turn an regular VR or AR revel in right into a extra compelling and enjoyable one. By encouraging exploration and interaction, customers are motivated to engage greater deeply with the virtual environment. Interactive narratives, in which customers could make decisions or form the course of activities, can further decorate this sense of involvement. The potential to influence the virtual world makes the enjoy extra dynamic and personalized, for that reason improving user engagement.

Personalization is any other important component. Allowing users to customise their avatars, choose their surroundings, or adjust the digital space gives them a experience of possession over the experience. This level of personalization could make users experience more connected to the environment, which in flip can improve their typical revel in. It additionally adds to the sensation that the digital world isn't always simply a place to passively look at but one which they can actively shape.

Ensuring accessibility is also paramount. A VR or AR enjoy that isn't on hand can alienate big segments of the potential consumer base. To deal with this, builders must offer flexible manage alternatives, inclusive of gesture-based controls or voice commands, that cater to humans with unique capabilities. Additionally, cognitive and sensory considerations should be taken into account—designing digital spaces with adjustable visual elements for colour blindness, or ensuring that audio content material is accompanied through text captions, can make the revel in extra inclusive. Accessibility also includes providing options for human beings with physical limitations, which include customizable manage schemes or much less bodily demanding interactions.

Realism is a key issue of immersion in both VR and AR. The greater sensible a digital surroundings feels, the much more likely it's miles to draw users in. Achieving a excessive stage of realism calls for attention to element, from realistic textures and lights to sensible physics and interactions. The visual fidelity of an environment performs a significant role, however so does the smaller, greater diffused components— ambient sounds, environmental noise, and the behaviors of digital gadgets. For instance, while customers have interaction with an item in a virtual space, it ought to behave in a realistic way: if it's miles picked up, moved, or thrown, its reaction ought to mimic that of a real-global object. Realism is not confined to visuals; even the way characters or factors react to person input can make a vast distinction in how believable the environment feels.

However, builders ought to additionally keep away from overwhelming customers with sensory enter. Too many stimuli can confuse or frustrate the consumer, inflicting them to disengage. Striking a balance among rich, attractive visuals and ease is key to maintaining immersion. For instance, at the same time as it's important to consist of detailed visuals in digital areas, overly complicated interfaces or chaotic movements can disrupt the user's attention. A well-designed digital world introduces new factors progressively, allowing customers time to technique the information and live engaged with out feeling overloaded.

Lastly, social interplay in VR and AR environments can significantly beautify the enjoy. Social interaction no longer handiest makes virtual worlds extra attractive however additionally fosters a experience of connection and community. Whether customers are interacting with others in a multiplayer game or participating on a shared task, social functions can enhance immersion and make the experience sense greater actual. Allowing users to customise their avatars and providing intuitive verbal exchange tools—including voice chat or gesture recognition—further enriches those interactions. The capability to interact with different customers in real-time creates a dynamic, evolving experience that provides a layer of intensity and emotional connection.

Enhancing user experience in VR and AR involves a thoughtful aggregate of seamless interaction, consolation, engaging content material, accessibility, realism, and social interplay. By carefully thinking about those aspects, developers can create reviews that are not simplest immersive and enjoyable but additionally long-lasting and significant. These factors work collectively to make certain that customers experience connected to the digital world in a manner that is each intuitive and deeply attractive, retaining them coming again for extra.

CHAPTER 6

The Future of Digital Twins

6.1. The Future Role of Virtual Reality and Augmented Reality

The rapid evolution of era has already begun to redefine the limits of what we perceive because the bodily global, and Virtual Reality (VR) and Augmented Reality (AR) are at the forefront of this transformation. As we look toward the future, these technologies will play an an increasing number of widespread role in bridging the distance between the real and digital worlds, growing significant possibilities throughout various sectors, such as business, healthcare, training, and leisure.

Virtual Reality and Augmented Reality, whilst integrated with Digital Twins, can catalyze a wholly new paradigm for both interaction and information of the world. These technologies will allow companies, institutions, and people to revel in their bodily counterparts clearly, with extra accuracy and intensity. The evolution of VR and AR technologies will enable us to explore, manipulate, and simulate complicated systems and environments that might in any other case be inaccessible or too high-priced to have interaction with.

As we progress into the destiny, one of the key roles VR and AR will play is in enhancing the realism and precision of Digital Twins. By the usage of VR, customers might be able to immerse themselves in virtual replicas of physical environments, experiencing them in a fully interactive and 3-

dimensional way. The capacity to visualize and control a digital dual in a simulated international will allow industries which include architecture, urban making plans, and production to optimize their designs earlier than they are realized in the actual global. In healthcare, VR will permit scientific experts to engage with patients' virtual replicas, aiding in more correct diagnoses and customized remedy plans.

The destiny of VR and AR may also result in full-size advancements in actual-time data integration. As VR and AR technology enhance, they will permit for seamless integration with IoT (Internet of Things) sensors and actual-time analytics, that allows you to provide a good extra accurate and dynamic illustration of bodily gadgets and environments. This will allow agencies to higher reveal, control, and optimize operations in actual time. For instance, in a production plant, a Digital Twin powered with the aid of AR should provide employees with visible instructions or remarks, permitting them to make instant adjustments to equipment or methods based totally on real-time records, thereby improving efficiency and reducing errors.

Another main development within the destiny of VR and AR could be the capacity to scale Digital Twins in new ways. Instead of focusing entirely on person components or strategies, destiny technologies will permit for the advent of town-scale or even international-scale Digital Twins. This will revolutionize industries like city making plans and environmental management. Cities may be digitally replicated, permitting planners to test with extraordinary infrastructure situations, transportation fashions, and environmental situations to optimize using resources and predict the effect of diverse guidelines or adjustments. This could even make bigger to weather modeling, wherein VR and AR technology can be used to simulate the impact of climate alternate and plan mitigation strategies greater successfully.

In education, the destiny of VR and AR will beautify how we study the world around us. With immersive VR environments, students could be able to discover the internal workings of the human frame, have interaction with historic activities, or even visit remote planets—all from the consolation of their study room. Digital Twins incorporated with VR may want to take this similarly, imparting college students with an opportunity to engage with special, updated fashions of ecosystems, machines, or historical systems in approaches that were in no way before viable. This immersive enjoy will foster a deeper understanding of complicated structures, making gaining knowledge of each extra engaging and extra effective.

For agencies, VR and AR will hold to redefine how products and services are advertised, sold, and supported. By allowing customers to experience merchandise in immersive environments, companies will be capable of provide personalised, interactive experiences that enhance customer engagement. Virtual showrooms, where customers can test out merchandise in a simulated environment, will become not unusual. Furthermore, AR packages may be used to create actual-time, contextual records overlays, allowing customers to view additional product details, specs, or tutorials when they interact with bodily products.

One of the maximum interesting possibilities of VR and AR integration with Digital Twins lies within the healthcare zone. Virtual reality's capacity to create immersive environments, combined with the detailed simulations provided through virtual twins, can rework each patient care and medical schooling. Surgeons can practice strategies in particularly practical, virtual environments, gaining revel in with none danger to actual patients. Digital twins of organs or entire human bodies, made from medical imaging records, will allow medical doctors to simulate surgeries and treatment plans to determine the first-rate direction of motion for each affected person. These technologies will also permit for the simulation of disorder development, permitting healthcare carriers to provide extra correct diagnoses and predictive insights into ability health problems.

Moreover, VR and AR technologies will serve to decorate collaboration. Remote paintings, already a growing fashion, can be taken to the subsequent degree via the usage of immersive VR meeting rooms. These digital areas will permit teams to collaborate in actual-time, irrespective of their geographical locations. By combining Digital Twins with VR or

AR, teams will be capable of view and manage digital representations of complex tasks, whether it's a design blueprint, a statistics set, or a physical product, fostering extra effective collaboration.

In the amusement industry, VR and AR will hold to offer new stories that push the bounds of storytelling. Games, films, and immersive reports becomes greater interactive, engaging, and customizable. With the combination of Digital Twins, future VR studies may want to provide life like simulations of real-global environments that customers can navigate in immersive detail. Additionally, AR will permit for the blending of digital elements into the real global, reworking the way we revel in media through providing immersive, interactive narratives that respond to the consumer's actions and movements.

The destiny of VR and AR technologies may also involve tremendous enhancements in hardware. As headset designs grow to be lighter, extra cushty, and more cheap, the barrier to access for each customers and agencies will retain to lower. Furthermore, upgrades in processing power and visual fidelity will create even greater realistic reports, permitting more sophisticated applications of Digital Twins in industries along with structure, automobile design, and urban development. Augmented fact gadgets will preserve to conform from smartphones and clever glasses to extra specialised wearable devices, making it easier to get admission to virtual information in actual-world settings.

The position of VR and AR within the destiny will no longer be confined to the practical programs of business and healthcare. These technology will even redefine how we engage with art, way of life, and society. With Digital Twins, digital representations of ancient websites, cultural artifacts, and art installations will allow people to interact with and preserve cultural heritage in unheard of ways. Visitors should discover historical ruins in VR or view masterpieces in AR, reworking how museums and cultural institutions have interaction with the general public. These immersive reviews may also permit humans to discover new varieties of artwork, inclusive of virtual sculptures, performances, and interactive installations that exist only in the digital realm.

The future position of Virtual Reality and Augmented Reality together with Digital Twins is considered one of big capability. As those technologies hold to adapt, they'll reshape the way we recognize and have interaction with each the physical and digital worlds. Whether for schooling, business, healthcare, entertainment, or artwork, VR and AR will provide a brand new degree of engagement, providing studies that aren't most effective immersive and practical however also transformative.

6.2. Evolution and Predictions for Digital Twins

The idea of Digital Twins has hastily superior from an abstract perception to a powerful technological tool that is remodeling industries international. The evolution of Digital Twins has been pushed through improvements in various fields, which includes the Internet of Things (IoT), records analytics, artificial intelligence (AI), and cloud computing. These technologies have not best made it feasible to create an increasing number of state-of-the-art virtual replicas of bodily systems but additionally allowed for real-time tracking, evaluation, and optimization.

The adventure of Digital Twins started with simple representations of bodily property, along with engines or machines, where engineers may want to music the overall performance of character additives through sensors and software program. Over time, this concept accelerated to embody whole structures, facilities, cities, and even complicated networks. The early adoption of Digital Twins became specifically confined to manufacturing, where the generation helped corporations optimize operations, improve performance, and predict equipment screw ups before they came about. Today, however, Digital Twins have unfold to a wide variety of sectors, together with healthcare, construction, city making plans, and energy control, with their packages becoming more and more complex and integrated.

Looking closer to the future, the evolution of Digital Twins is poised to herald even greater profound adjustments. One of the most sizable trends is the increasing complexity of the virtual models. As technologies like AI and device learning keep to enhance, Digital Twins will become capable of self-learning, adapting to adjustments within the bodily international autonomously. This ought to lead to the development of "self sufficient Digital Twins" that not most effective mirror physical items or procedures but additionally expect future outcomes and make recommendations for optimization without human intervention. These advancements can be specifically beneficial in sectors like autonomous motors, smart towns, and healthcare, where actual-time decision-making is essential.

In the world of commercial packages, Digital Twins will evolve to deal with large, extra intricate structures. Manufacturing corporations will more and more use virtual twins to model whole production traces or entire factories, offering a complete view of operations. Real-time records from IoT sensors and AI analytics will enable companies to perform predictive renovation, optimize workflows, and even simulate one-of-a-kind production eventualities earlier than enforcing adjustments within the actual international. The aggregate of Digital Twins with augmented fact (AR) will further decorate this functionality, permitting people to interact with digital replicas of bodily systems without delay within their environment.

Another key evolution will be the integration of Digital Twins with edge computing. Edge computing brings computation closer to the supply of data, lowering latency and enabling quicker selection-making. By leveraging part computing, Digital Twins will be capable of procedure statistics in real-time at the site of operation, as opposed to depending completely on cloud-based totally processing. This may be specially beneficial in environments where short response instances are vital, which includes in independent motors or commercial manage systems.

Urban planning and clever cities will see large advancements as Digital Twins come to be extra state-of-the-art. Cities are already the use of Digital Twins to model infrastructure, site visitors structures, and environmental elements. In the destiny, these models turns into more granular, incorporating the whole lot from character buildings and roads to energy grids and water structures. Real-time data from IoT devices scattered at some point of the metropolis will feed into these virtual replicas, allowing town planners to display visitors congestion, optimize public transportation routes, or maybe are expecting the effect of environmental adjustments on city infrastructure. As towns evolve, their Digital Twins will become imperative to their operation, guiding everything from urban development to emergency response making plans.

Healthcare is every other sector in which Digital Twins are poised to make significant strides. In the approaching years, customized healthcare might be revolutionized thru the usage of man or woman Digital Twins. These models, produced from a affected person's clinical information, genetic facts, and actual-time fitness tracking, will permit medical doctors to simulate ability treatment effects, expect sickness progression, and tailor customized care plans for sufferers. The integration of AI and machine mastering into healthcare Digital Twins may also enhance the rate and accuracy of diagnoses, making healthcare greater proactive rather than reactive.

As the skills of Digital Twins develop, their role in environmental management will even amplify. From monitoring pollutants degrees in actual-time to modeling the effects of weather exchange, Digital Twins will become critical gear for dealing with natural resources and mitigating the affects of worldwide warming. By simulating complete ecosystems or climate systems, scientists might be able to are expecting and examine the effect of diverse environmental regulations earlier than they're implemented. This will be a game-changer for industries which include agriculture, forestry, and strength, wherein sustainability is becoming an an increasing number of critical subject.

The improvement of Digital Twins may even have profound implications for the combination of synthetic intelligence. As AI maintains to boost, it will be used to decorate the abilties of Digital Twins, allowing them to autonomously hit upon anomalies, optimize systems, and are expecting destiny behaviors. The synergy between AI and Digital Twins may be particularly impactful in fields like manufacturing and logistics, where predictive abilties are important for minimizing downtime and enhancing performance.

Moreover, as 5G networks turn out to be more widespread, the performance of Digital Twins will be stronger. With 5G's potential to transmit data at lightning-fast speeds and with minimum latency, Digital Twins will be capable of receive and system actual-time statistics from IoT gadgets more successfully, enabling close to-immediately updates. This could be vital in packages which includes clever towns, self sufficient vehicles, and far off healthcare tracking, in which real-time responsiveness is critical.

One of the most thrilling elements of the future of Digital Twins is their capacity for pass-enterprise collaboration. The integration of records from numerous sectors into a unified Digital Twin version will allow industries to collaborate in approaches that were formerly not possible. For example, the combination of transportation information from the automobile industry with infrastructure statistics from city planning may want to lead to the introduction of a comprehensive Digital Twin of a whole transportation community. This could permit for the optimization of the entirety from site visitors waft to automobile protection.

As Digital Twins come to be greater pervasive, the moral and safety worries associated with their use can even end up more pressing. With sizable quantities of personal, economic, and operational information being gathered and analyzed, the privateness and protection of this facts will want to be safeguarded. Furthermore, as Digital Twins end up more self sustaining, questions on accountability and choice-making will stand up. It will be essential for policymakers and enterprise leaders to set up clear recommendations and policies to control the usage of this generation, making sure it's far used responsibly and ethically.

The evolution of Digital Twins is poised to retain at an increased tempo, with new advancements in AI, IoT, and statistics analytics using their development. The technology will preserve to beautify industries starting from manufacturing to healthcare, supplying more and more state-of-the-art equipment for real-time tracking, optimization, and choice-making. The future of Digital Twins could be characterized with the aid of extra integration with different technology, which include AR and aspect computing, in addition to the growth in their abilities into new sectors like environmental management and clever cities. As these virtual replicas end up greater shrewd, interconnected, and self sufficient, they'll unlock new possibilities for industries, individuals, and society as a whole.

6.3. Potential Impacts on Society and Business

The fast evolution and vast adoption of Digital Twins promise profound adjustments throughout numerous sectors, with some distance-reaching implications for each society and commercial enterprise. As those virtual replicas turn out to be extra sophisticated, their impact will extend into nearly every factor of modern lifestyles, reworking how we interact with the physical global, make choices, and solve troubles. From improving efficiency in agencies to reshaping societal systems, the ability affects of Digital Twins are tremendous.

In the enterprise international, Digital Twins are already revolutionizing industries by improving operational performance, decreasing expenses, and allowing more precise decision-making. The capability to create a virtual replica of a bodily gadget permits agencies to display, analyze, and optimize their operations in actual time. For example, producers use Digital Twins to simulate production strategies, reveal the overall performance of system, and are expecting whilst preservation is wanted, in the end main to decreased downtime and stepped forward productivity. In the coming years, the combination of AI and device gaining knowledge of will enhance these talents, permitting companies to expect destiny tendencies, automate decision-making, and even optimize entire deliver chains without human intervention. This shift in the direction of independent operations will lessen the want for manual oversight, lower operational charges, and improve the general efficiency of businesses.

The potential to simulate and optimize techniques in a virtual surroundings will also empower groups to experiment with new enterprise fashions and products with out the threat and price related to physical trials. For instance, in industries such as automotive or aerospace, agencies can create digital prototypes of new vehicles or aircraft, take a look at their performance in a variety of situations, and make adjustments before constructing the bodily product. This will shorten development cycles, reduce fees, and allow groups to innovate extra rapidly.

Moreover, Digital Twins will permit businesses to enhance client experiences through offering greater customized and tailor-made offerings. By studying facts from real-global interactions, groups can create digital replicas of person clients, allowing them to offer particularly custom designed products and services. In the retail area, as an instance, Digital Twins could be used to tune purchaser alternatives and behaviors, allowing agencies to deliver more centered marketing campaigns and product guidelines. This stage of personalization will enhance purchaser pleasure and loyalty, using commercial enterprise boom.

For the broader society, the large adoption of Digital Twins should result in extra connectivity and efficiency in urban environments. Smart cities, powered by means of Digital Twins, will leverage real-time information from sensors embedded throughout urban infrastructure to optimize the whole thing from site visitors float to power consumption. By simulating the effects of various guidelines or adjustments to the city environment, city planners can make greater knowledgeable selections that enhance first-rate of lifestyles for citizens. For example, visitors styles may be monitored in real-time, and digital models of the town's transportation infrastructure may be adjusted to lessen congestion or improve public shipping routes. Similarly, power structures can be optimized by way of growing digital replicas of power grids, making an allowance for better management of sources and reduced power waste.

The integration of Digital Twins into healthcare will have transformative effects on hospital therapy and public health. As healthcare structures continue to adopt these technology, sufferers will gain from more customized and proactive care. Digital Twins of individuals, made out of their clinical statistics, genetic statistics, and real-time fitness records, will allow docs to expect health problems earlier than they rise up, take a look at extraordinary treatment alternatives, or even simulate ability results. This will cause extra powerful treatments, quicker recovery instances, and a reduction in healthcare prices. Moreover, the potential to simulate the impact of environmental factors on public health will allow governments and businesses to higher prepare for pandemics or sickness outbreaks, leading to advanced global health management.

At a societal stage, the full-size use of Digital Twins may want to create new activity possibilities and ability sets. As organizations and industries adopt those technologies, call for for workers skilled in regions such as statistics analysis, AI, gadget getting to know, and virtual modeling will growth. New industries and process roles centered on the development, protection, and application of Digital Twins will emerge, imparting tremendous opportunities for employment and economic increase. However, this shift may also lead to job displacement for workers whose roles are automated with the aid of Digital Twin generation. As a end result, society will need to address the ability for process loss with the aid of investing in retraining and upskilling projects to assist employees transition to new roles.

On the alternative hand, the full-size implementation of Digital Twins increases numerous societal and moral concerns that must be addressed. One of the most pressing issues is facts privateness. The creation of digital replicas relies on the gathering and evaluation of tremendous quantities of private and touchy records, which includes medical information, economic transactions, and behavioral patterns. Ensuring the safety of this data and defensive people' privacy could be important to keeping agree with in Digital Twin generation. Regulatory frameworks will want to be evolved to make sure that records is gathered and used responsibly, with strict suggestions on consent, get admission to, and records sharing.

Another problem is the capability for Digital Twins to exacerbate existing inequalities. As Digital Twins become fundamental to industries which includes healthcare, training, and finance, there is a threat that positive agencies might not have identical get admission to to those technologies. Those with limited get admission to to era, whether or not due to financial, geographic, or social barriers, might be left at the back of in a world increasingly more driven by way of Digital Twins. Ensuring equitable get admission to to these technology could be critical to save you the advent of a digital divide and make sure that the advantages of Digital Twins are shared with the aid of all individuals of society.

In addition to these issues, the growing reliance on Digital Twins for decision-making could enhance questions about responsibility and duty. As Digital Twins grow to be extra independent, with AI structures making choices based on real-time facts and simulations, it is able to come to be unclear who is in the long run responsible while some thing is going wrong. In the occasion of a failure or mistakes, such as an business coincidence or a healthcare mishap, figuring out liability can be complicated. Legal frameworks will want to conform to address these new challenges and ensure that individuals and organizations are held answerable for the moves of virtual systems.

While Digital Twins hold terrific capability to transform business operations and improve societal functioning, their adoption additionally comes with demanding situations that have to be carefully navigated. As industries include this generation, they may free up new opportunities for efficiency, innovation, and consumer satisfaction. At the equal time, society have to address issues associated with statistics privateness, fairness, and duty to make certain that the blessings of Digital Twins are found out in a accountable and inclusive manner. The destiny of Digital Twins might be formed now not handiest by way of technological improvements however also via the ethical and societal decisions made nowadays.

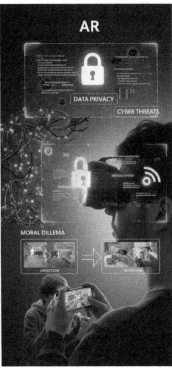

CHAPTER 7

Ethical and Security Issues in Virtual Reality and Augmented Reality

7.1. Issues of Privacy and Security

As digital truth (VR) and augmented truth (AR) technologies keep to conform and combine extra deeply into diverse elements of each day existence, issues regarding privacy and protection have come to be essential. These technology gather widespread quantities of private statistics, starting from biometric data and physical actions to private options and interactions inside digital spaces. While the potential for immersive reviews and innovation is vast, those technology also introduce enormous dangers to man or woman privacy and facts safety, which want to be addressed as they retain to broaden.

In terms of privacy, VR and AR systems have the ability to gather certain data approximately customers' behaviors, physical surroundings, or even emotional states. For instance, VR headsets can music eye moves and facial expressions to regulate the content material, developing a customized experience. Similarly, AR devices, together with smart glasses or cell AR programs, frequently use cameras and sensors to test the user's surroundings in actual time. This regular monitoring raises significant privateness worries, as non-public statistics is continuously being gathered and potentially shared without explicit person consent.

The facts amassed with the aid of VR and AR structures also can be deeply touchy. Eye-monitoring information, as an example, can monitor a lot approximately someone's emotional reactions, choices, and even intellectual state. Similarly, facial popularity generation, frequently utilized in AR applications for interplay and authentication, can save biometric records that can be exploited if accessed by malicious events. As users interact with virtual environments, the threat of inadvertently sharing non-public or private information will increase, specially if there's insufficient transparency approximately what statistics is being accrued and how it is being used.

Additionally, VR and AR technologies can blur the line between the real and digital worlds, leading to new privacy challenges. For instance, AR programs may also use place data to overlay digital records onto the user's physical environment. While this creates a continuing enjoy, it also manner that the person's area is being constantly tracked. If this facts is not properly covered, it may be accessed by using third parties, along with advertisers, authorities corporations, or malicious actors, ensuing in capability misuse.

The collection and use of this records are frequently compounded via the lack of clear guidelines and standards governing VR and AR technology. Privacy policies for these technology might not be as comprehensive as the ones for more conventional styles of statistics series, leaving clients unsure about the extent of information amassed and how it is blanketed. The absence of a global framework for statistics privateness within the VR and AR area makes it more tough to shield users' rights and make certain they have got manage over their non-public facts.

In addition to privacy concerns, protection is another primary difficulty in the VR and AR ecosystems. As with any virtual platform, there may be the threat of cyberattacks, hacking, and records breaches. VR and AR gadgets rely upon internet connections to deliver content and enable actual-time interactions, creating opportunities for malicious actors to gain unauthorized get admission to to users' devices and statistics. For example, attackers should take advantage of vulnerabilities in VR or AR systems to install malware, scouse borrow non-public data, or even manipulate virtual environments to cause harm.

Moreover, the immersive nature of VR and AR reviews can introduce new protection dangers. In the case of VR, users are often absolutely immersed in a virtual environment, which may additionally make it hard for them to notice capability threats or malicious interest taking place inside the historical past. This can go away customers vulnerable to hacking, identity theft, or maybe psychological manipulation. In AR, where digital factors are overlaid onto the actual world, attackers may want to probably take advantage of those digital overlays to mislead customers or manage the physical environment. For instance, an attacker may want to modify digital objects in an AR game to misinform the player or purpose them to have interaction with dangerous physical items.

The safety dangers are further compounded by means of the usage of cloud-primarily based services in VR and AR packages. Many VR and AR platforms shop person statistics and interactions on far off servers, making it extra vulnerable to statistics breaches. If those cloud servers are compromised, touchy user records—which include login credentials, payment statistics, and private options—may be uncovered. The reliance on cloud infrastructure also raises issues about the ability lack of control over user information, as it is able to be tough for people to fully recognize where their statistics is being stored and who has get right of entry to to it.

Another critical attention is the security of virtual assets, specifically in the context of VR and AR-based video games or platforms that involve digital economies. With the rise of virtual worlds, customers often buy, exchange, or even create virtual items, which are stored inside those platforms. These assets, which includes virtual currencies, apparel for avatars, or virtual property, have real-global value and may be focused by means of cybercriminals. Hackers might also attempt to thieve digital goods, manage in-recreation economies, or disrupt transactions, leading to financial losses and a loss of trust inside the safety of those platforms.

To deal with these privateness and protection demanding situations, it is important that VR and AR builders prioritize the implementation of strong security features and privateness policies. This consists of making sure that users' data is securely encrypted, imparting transparency about what statistics is being accrued, and imparting users manage over their non-public facts. Strong authentication techniques, which include multi-issue authentication, have to also be used to protect user accounts from unauthorized get right of entry to. Additionally, developers need to layout structures that permit users to opt-out of statistics collection in which viable and offer clean, easily comprehensible privacy settings.

Regulatory bodies will also need to play a key function in addressing the privacy and protection worries surrounding VR and AR technology. As those technology maintain to proliferate, governments have to paintings to set up and enforce statistics protection policies especially tailored to the VR and AR sectors. This may additionally involve developing new law that governs how private facts is dealt with, as well as imposing industry requirements for cybersecurity. International collaboration might be necessary to make sure that privateness and safety requirements are regular throughout borders and that customers can experience assured that their statistics is covered, irrespective of where they're positioned.

While VR and AR technologies provide exciting possibilities for innovation and enjoyment, they also introduce substantial privateness and security dangers. As these technologies retain to conform and come to be incorporated into daily existence, it's miles important that builders, policymakers, and customers work collectively to make sure that privacy is blanketed and security dangers are minimized. By imposing sturdy security features, adhering to transparent statistics privateness practices, and setting up clear regulatory frameworks, the VR and AR industries can preserve to thrive whilst safeguarding customers' private information and making sure their safety in those immersive virtual environments.

7.2. Addiction and Psychological Effects

As digital fact (VR) and augmented fact (AR) technology end up extra immersive and handy, there is developing concern about their ability to purpose addiction and psychological outcomes in users. These technology offer an extraordinary level of engagement, permitting individuals to revel in digital worlds that intently resemble reality, once in a while blurring the strains between the 2. While VR and AR have enormous nice applications in regions like amusement, education, and remedy, their immersive nature can also result in negative consequences, in particular whilst overused or misused. Understanding the mental effect of these technology is crucial for mitigating potential risks and ensuring that they may be used responsibly.

One of the number one concerns related to VR and AR technology is their capability for dependancy. Similar to different virtual platforms, such as video games and social media, VR and AR reports are designed to captivate users, encouraging them to spend extended durations of time in digital environments. The relatively immersive nature of VR, in particular, can create a experience of escapism, in which users lose song of time and end up deeply worried in the virtual worlds they inhabit. For a few, this may cause compulsive utilization patterns, in which they choose virtual studies over real-life interactions and obligations.

The concept of "flow"—a psychological state wherein individuals are absolutely immersed in an pastime and revel in a experience of leisure and pride—can be effortlessly prompted in VR and AR environments. This state of complete absorption can be useful in certain contexts, consisting of getting to know or creative work. However, whilst taken to extremes, it can turn out to be problematic. Users can also experience an irresistible pull to go back to virtual worlds, particularly if those environments offer rewards, demanding situations, or social interactions which can be more satisfying than their actual-international counterparts. This sort of conduct can lead to neglect of critical factors of each day existence, which include paintings, relationships, and physical health.

In addition to addiction, prolonged publicity to VR and AR can have vast psychological effects, particularly when used excessively. One of the maximum concerning potential influences is the blurring of obstacles between the virtual and the real. When people spend large amounts of time in VR or

AR environments, they will start to lose their sense of truth. This disconnection can cause feelings of misunderstanding, disorientation, or even derealization, wherein the person feels indifferent from the actual global. In severe instances, people may enjoy trouble distinguishing among digital stories and actual events, which could cause emotional distress and challenges in processing actual-international situations.

The psychological outcomes of VR and AR aren't restricted to customers' belief of fact. There also are worries about how these technology can have an impact on conduct and emotional nicely-being. For instance, studies has proven that folks who have interaction in violent VR games or studies may come to be desensitized to violent conduct in real lifestyles. The immersive nature of VR makes these digital experiences sense more sensible, which can intensify emotional reactions and enhance poor behaviors. In AR, the mixing of digital factors into the actual global can modify users' perceptions of their surroundings, leading to potential anxiety or discomfort, particularly if the digital overlays are perceived as intrusive or disruptive.

Another psychological impact is the ability for social isolation. While VR and AR technology offer new avenues for social interaction—such as multiplayer video games, digital meetups, and digital social areas—they also can make a contribution to a reduction in face-to-face socialization. As people become extra immersed in digital worlds, they will begin to prioritize on line interactions over actual-lifestyles relationships. This shift can result in emotions of loneliness, despair, and social withdrawal, specially if digital connections update authentic human touch. The social dynamics within virtual environments can occasionally be shallow or artificial, which may additionally exacerbate feelings of isolation and reduce the overall first-rate of social reviews.

Additionally, VR and AR studies can create a heightened feel of immersion which can affect intellectual fitness in both superb and negative ways. On the only hand, these technology were shown to provide healing blessings, which includes decreasing anxiety or ache in sure scientific contexts. For example, VR has been used in publicity therapy to assist people confront phobias, or in ache management to distract patients all through scientific processes. However, excessive use or poorly designed experiences may additionally exacerbate pre-present mental fitness situations. Users who are already struggling with anxiety, depression, or other mental disorders might also find that VR and AR exacerbate their signs and symptoms as opposed to alleviate them. The depth of the digital studies ought to extend bad emotions, making it difficult for customers to regulate their intellectual nation.

Another trouble to take into account is the ability for "simulation illness" or "cybersickness," that's a shape of motion illness that could occur whilst users enjoy a disconnect between their visual belief in a virtual environment and their physical sensations. This circumstance can cause signs and symptoms including nausea, dizziness, headaches, and fatigue. While those consequences are not universally skilled by all users, they may be debilitating for a few, in particular with prolonged use of VR headsets. The psychological pain as a result of simulation illness can deter people from the use of VR generation, hindering its capacity for fantastic applications and studies.

To mitigate the risks associated with addiction and psychological results, it is critical that VR and AR developers, healthcare specialists, and educators collaborate to create guidelines for accountable utilization. One capacity answer is the implementation of usage limits or "time-outs," encouraging customers to take regular breaks from virtual environments to save you overuse. This ought to assist keep a healthy balance among digital and real-international studies. Developers ought to additionally layout VR and AR studies that sell properly-being, including incorporating capabilities that inspire physical hobby or social interplay in meaningful methods.

Furthermore, users must be knowledgeable approximately the ability psychological risks of VR and AR, especially regarding the significance of balancing display time with actual-world sports. By elevating recognition of the mental effects, users could make greater informed choices approximately how and when to interact with these technologies. Parents and educators, particularly, play a key function in tracking and guiding younger customers to ensure that VR and AR technology are used in a wholesome, accountable manner.

While virtual truth and augmented fact provide sizable ability for innovation and positive alternate, they also introduce tremendous risks in terms of dependancy and psychological outcomes. The immersive nature of these technology can result in compulsive behavior, disorientation, and bad influences on mental fitness if not used carefully. By taking proactive steps to deal with these concerns, such as promoting balanced usage, designing nicely-being-centered reviews, and teaching users about potential dangers, we will ensure that VR and AR technology are used responsibly and retain to provide benefits without inflicting harm to people' intellectual and emotional nicely-being.

7.3. Ethical Dilemmas and Responsibilities

7.3.1. Privacy Issues in Digital Twins

The idea of Digital Twins, which includes developing digital replicas of physical objects, structures, or environments, has notably extended the opportunities in diverse sectors together with production, healthcare, and concrete planning. However, as those virtual representations of the real global become more and more state-of-the-art, they introduce severe privateness issues that have to be cautiously controlled.

At the coronary heart of privateness issues in Digital Twins is the massive amount of records that is accumulated, processed, and stored. These digital replicas depend upon actual-time information from sensors, machines, or individuals to mirror their physical counterparts. For example, in a clever city version, a Digital Twin of a city's infrastructure may monitor the whole lot from site visitors styles and pollution levels to strength consumption and waste control. The statistics amassed can consist of private facts, from the area of people to their behaviors, alternatives, and even fitness metrics.

One of the maximum significant worries is the capacity for unauthorized get admission to to this sensitive records. With Digital Twins representing real-world environments which might be continually up to date with actual-time facts, they emerge as top goals for cyberattacks. Hackers should exploit vulnerabilities to gain access to personal records, that may lead to identity theft, monetary loss, or even bodily harm if vital infrastructure structures are compromised.

Furthermore, using Digital Twins in sectors like healthcare or retail additionally increases worries about consent and records ownership. In healthcare, Digital Twins can be used to model man or woman sufferers' situations, simulating capacity outcomes of different treatments. While this may lead to extra correct diagnostics and better patient care, it also affords the risk of individuals' fitness information being misused, shared with out right consent, or bought to third parties for commercial advantage. The proprietors of the records—the individuals whose personal information is being amassed—can also have restrained control over how it is used, stored, or shared.

Another component of privateness worries in Digital Twins entails the stability between innovation and character rights. While the records collected via Digital Twins can drive advancements in era, medicine, and concrete making plans, it's miles crucial to ensure that privacy laws and ethical requirements are in area to save you the exploitation of personal statistics. Without proper regulation, the capacity for virtual surveillance becomes all too actual, in which humans may also unknowingly turn out to be subjects of non-stop monitoring.

As Digital Twin era progresses, it will become more and more important to create frameworks that shield the privateness of individuals while nonetheless taking into account the advancement of the generation. Clear tips need to be set up concerning consent, transparency, and facts ownership. Furthermore, using encryption, secure facts storage, and get admission to manipulate mechanisms can be essential in mitigating the risks associated with unauthorized records breaches.

The moral duty of these developing and imposing Digital Twin technology lies in ensuring that privacy is maintained, that people' rights are respected, and that the generation is used for the extra good without infringing on non-public freedoms.

7.3.2. Making Ethical Decisions in Virtual Worlds

The growing incidence of digital worlds, fueled via the advancements in virtual truth (VR) and augmented reality (AR), has delivered a number of ethical challenges. As those virtual environments grow to be more immersive and difficult, they more and more mirror actual-global reports, presenting unique moral dilemmas that require careful thought and responsible action. Ethical choices in virtual worlds move past simple issues of gameplay or entertainment; they encompass troubles associated with the remedy of avatars, social dynamics, privateness, or even the impact on actual-global behavior.

One key location of difficulty in digital worlds is the conduct and treatment of avatars, which represent individuals in these areas. Avatars regularly serve as extensions of a user's identity, and their interactions in the virtual surroundings can reflect or amplify behaviors visible inside the real world. In many digital environments, customers have the liberty to specific themselves, but this freedom frequently raises ethical questions about respect, consent, and boundaries. For instance, in multiplayer on line video games or social VR structures, users may additionally stumble upon harassment, bullying, or hate speech, which poses a vast moral dilemma for each the customers involved and the developers chargeable for the platform. Ensuring a safe, respectful, and inclusive area calls for the implementation of clear behavioral hints, moderation systems, and powerful enforcement of these guidelines to shield customers from harm.

In addition to interpersonal conduct, ethical questions additionally arise regarding the layout and purpose of virtual worlds. As VR and AR technology evolve, digital environments can more and more simulate actual-world situations, blurring the lines between fiction and fact. This raises the difficulty of virtual global creators' obligations—particularly in terms of designing content material this is potentially harmful. For example, builders would possibly design games or reports that characteristic violence, exploitation, or different immoral acts. These environments will have giant influences on users' conduct and attitudes, mainly while uncovered to such content material over lengthy durations of time. The moral query here is whether or not designers have a moral responsibility to recall the mental and emotional outcomes of such content material and whether they must exercise warning in allowing positive varieties of behavior or interactions within virtual spaces.

Another area of moral situation entails using personal records inside digital worlds. Just like in the actual international, digital environments accumulate large amounts of records about users, from their preferences and sports to extra touchy information such as behavioral patterns, facial expressions, or even physiological responses within the case of VR headsets. The collection and use of this data raise critical ethical questions about privateness, consent, and ownership. For instance, if users' information is accumulated without their informed consent or used for purposes beyond the scope of the virtual world they agreed to take part in, it constitutes an moral violation. This problem turns into more complicated when considering using records for targeted advertising and marketing, profiling, or selling to third events. Developers have to make sure that users are completely aware about how their information might be used and that they retain control over their private statistics. Transparent consent strategies, statistics safety rules, and consumer empowerment are vital to addressing those concerns.

Moreover, the increasing realism and interactivity of digital worlds raise concerns about their capability have an effect on on real-international behavior and ethics. As individuals immerse themselves in those virtual areas, their actions and stories inside those worlds can effect their real-world choices and attitudes. For example, a person who engages in competitive or violent conduct inside a virtual environment may additionally deliver the ones same behaviors into the physical global, challenging the long-debated query of whether or not exposure to virtual violence interprets into actual-international aggression. While studies in this connection stays ongoing, the moral obligation lies with both developers and users to foster advantageous, ethical behaviors in these virtual spaces, making sure that virtual worlds are designed and navigated in a way that promotes non-public boom and social responsibility.

Another vital thing of ethical selection-making in digital worlds is ensuring inclusivity and identical get admission to. Virtual worlds, particularly people who require full-size economic or technological investment, may inadvertently exclude positive corporations, leading to a loss of range in representation and participation. Ethical decisions have to be made to make sure that virtual environments are designed to be accessible to humans of all socioeconomic backgrounds, abilties, and cultural identities. This includes thinking about factors along with affordability, accessibility for humans with disabilities, and the promoting of diverse representation inside digital spaces.

As virtual worlds continue to grow in complexity and scale, the responsibility for making moral decisions will not relaxation solely on customers or developers, but additionally on governments and regulatory bodies. Policies and regulations will play a essential position in organising recommendations for moral conduct in digital environments, ensuring that digital areas continue to be safe, respectful, and conducive to positive engagement. Ethical frameworks need to be evolved to manual the design, regulation, and moderation of virtual worlds, and those frameworks need to evolve along technological advancements.

Making moral decisions in virtual worlds calls for a collaborative effort among all stakeholders concerned. Developers ought to design environments that prioritize recognize, consent, and inclusivity, while users should take into account in their movements and interactions inside those spaces. As virtual and augmented truth technologies keep to adapt, it's far vital that moral considerations remain at the vanguard in their development and use. By addressing those dilemmas proactively, we will make sure that digital worlds stay safe, enriching, and beneficial for all.

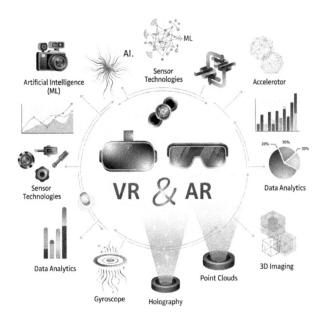

CHAPTER 8

Related Technologies and Advancements

8.1. Artificial Intelligence and Machine Learning

The rapid improvement of virtual and augmented fact (VR and AR) technology is carefully connected with advancements in artificial intelligence (AI) and gadget mastering (ML). As VR and AR push the boundaries of immersive experiences, AI and ML serve as crucial enablers, improving the functionality, realism, and interactivity of digital environments. Together, those technology are reshaping industries, permitting new opportunities for personalized stories, smart automation, and greater person interaction.

Artificial intelligence is the field of pc technological know-how that specializes in developing structures capable of acting duties that traditionally require human intelligence, along with expertise natural language, recognizing styles, and making decisions. In the context of VR and AR, AI performs a pivotal function in making digital environments extra responsive, interactive, and adaptive to the wishes of users.

For instance, AI-powered virtual retailers or characters can have interaction with users in a real looking manner, developing greater immersive and dynamic experiences. These AI marketers can research from their interactions with customers, adapting their responses based on previous behavior, choices, and even emotional cues. This creates a experience of realism in virtual spaces, wherein AI-pushed non-participant characters (NPCs) or avatars reply intelligently to customers' movements, making the environment feel more interactive and customized.

Moreover, AI is essential for processing the big amounts of facts that VR and AR systems generate in actual-time. For instance, AI algorithms can examine person behaviors, gestures, and moves, permitting VR and AR structures to modify thus. In AR, AI can assist apprehend and interpret the real-global environment, figuring out objects, places, and even faces to enhance the digital enjoy. This real-time processing and interaction are critical for presenting seamless and responsive VR and AR experiences.

Machine studying, a subset of AI, is a technique that lets in systems to study from statistics and improve through the years without being explicitly programmed. In the area of VR and AR, gadget gaining knowledge of algorithms enable structures to refine and personalize reviews based on person input, alternatives, and conduct.

In digital environments, gadget mastering may be used to create adaptive structures that evolve with the person. For example, system mastering fashions can analyze a person's interactions with a virtual environment and regulate the experience as a consequence. This would possibly consist of enhancing the difficulty of a game, tailoring the content or situations presented in an immersive schooling simulation, or offering personalised suggestions in VR social spaces. Through non-stop mastering, device studying algorithms allow these systems to improve their accuracy and effectiveness, making the reports more attractive and relevant to each character person.

In AR, device learning is vital for item recognition and spatial mapping. For example, AR applications can use system learning to perceive and track gadgets in the real global, covering virtual elements seamlessly onto bodily gadgets. This lets in for greater sophisticated and context-aware AR packages, from interactive marketing to superior industrial preservation, where the digital and actual-international factors ought to paintings in harmony.

Beyond improving person stories, AI and ML also are remodeling the way content is created within virtual and augmented environments. Traditional methods of creating VR and AR content material often require substantial human attempt, such as 3-D modeling, animation, and programming. AI and machine mastering have the potential to streamline those tactics, making content introduction greater green and on hand.

AI-pushed equipment can assist in automating positive factors of content material creation, which include generating sensible 3-D fashions, designing landscapes, or even animating characters. For instance, generative AI algorithms can create real looking textures and environments based totally on consumer inputs, notably lowering the time required for content manufacturing. In the context of AR, device gaining knowledge of can help in generating sensible holograms or digital gadgets that combine seamlessly with the actual international, based at the person's surroundings.

Machine getting to know can also enhance procedural content technology, a way utilized in gaming and digital global design to create massive, dynamic environments without guide intervention. Through the usage of gadget studying, virtual worlds can be dynamically generated and tailored to the consumer's behavior and options, developing precise reviews that evolve over the years.

One of the most extensive affects of AI and ML on VR and AR is within the area of training and simulation. Industries consisting of healthcare, aviation, army, and schooling are increasingly more leveraging VR and AR for immersive training packages that mirror actual-global scenarios in a safe and controlled digital area. The integration of AI and ML in addition complements those packages by using supplying adaptive mastering stories that evolve based totally on the person's performance.

In healthcare, as an example, AI-powered VR simulations allow scientific experts to exercise complicated surgical procedures or techniques in a danger-unfastened environment, with system getting to know algorithms tracking their performance and presenting comments. This permits for non-stop development and personalization of training packages. In the navy, VR and AR structures use AI to create sensible combat situations, adjusting the level of trouble or the conduct of simulated adversaries based totally at the trainee's capabilities and development. Such packages are not best improving the effectiveness of training however also making it extra price-green and scalable.

AI and ML are particularly powerful in improving healthcare packages inside VR and AR. Machine studying algorithms can analyze a patient's fitness facts to provide personalized pointers for rehabilitation, physical therapy, or ache control. In VR, AI-pushed simulations can create customized rehabilitation programs for sufferers recovering from injuries or surgeries, adjusting the depth of exercises based on their progress.

In AR, device studying can assist clinical experts throughout surgical procedures or diagnostics by means of providing actual-time overlays of vital records. For instance, AR glasses can undertaking designated scans of a patient's anatomy onto their frame during surgery, with AI algorithms analyzing the information and suggesting capacity interventions. This generation is remodeling the manner healthcare experts engage with sufferers, making clinical methods greater correct and less invasive.

Despite the great ability of AI and ML in improving VR and AR studies, their integration comes with numerous challenges and moral considerations. One situation is the information privateness and protection of users interacting with AI-driven digital environments. AI systems frequently depend on large datasets to teach machine getting to know fashions, which can include sensitive data approximately users' behaviors, alternatives, and even bodily health. Ensuring that this facts is treated securely and transparently is important to keeping accept as true with and shielding consumer privateness.

Another undertaking is the ability for bias in AI and device gaining knowledge of algorithms. Since those systems are skilled on historical records, they'll inadvertently replicate existing biases or inequalities. In VR and AR applications, this will manifest as biased decision-making, unfair treatment of sure users, or inaccurate representations of individuals from various backgrounds. Developers ought to be aware of these risks and paintings to create inclusive and honest AI structures that serve the needs of all customers.

Artificial intelligence and gadget getting to know are transforming virtual and augmented fact technologies, making them smarter, more customized, and more and more green. These technologies are improving person reports, streamlining content material introduction, and enabling groundbreaking packages in fields like healthcare, education, and entertainment. As VR and AR hold to conform, the combination of AI and ML may be vital in shaping the future of immersive digital environments. However, ethical concerns such as statistics privacy, security, and bias should be addressed to make certain those technologies are used responsibly and inclusively.

8.2. Sensor Technologies and Data Analytics

The intersection of sensor technologies and information analytics is one of the maximum transformative elements within the fields of virtual and augmented truth (VR and AR). These technology enable extra immersive and dynamic studies through offering real-time records about the bodily international, which can then be processed and incorporated into digital environments. The synergy among sensors and facts analytics underpins a few of the advances in VR, AR, and related technology, letting them be greater responsive, accurate, and customized.

At the center of both VR and AR are sensors that seize statistics from the bodily surroundings. These sensors play a vital function in tracking consumer interactions, detecting motion, and mapping the environment. In VR, sensors are used to tune the person's head moves, hand gestures, and body positions, allowing the digital international to react accordingly. In AR, sensors acquire records from the actual global, consisting of the region, orientation, and length of physical objects, to correctly overlay digital elements onto them.

Types of Sensors Used in VR and AR

1. Motion Sensors: Motion sensors, along with accelerometers, gyroscopes, and magnetometers, are essential for monitoring the movement of customers or devices in digital and augmented environments. These sensors enable structures to stumble on a user's physical actions and translate them into corresponding moves in the digital international, including looking around, taking walks, or interacting with digital objects. In VR headsets, motion sensors permit users to govern their movement within the virtual surroundings, developing a extra immersive and intuitive enjoy.

2. Depth Sensors: Depth sensors, such as LiDAR (Light Detection and Ranging), are essential in AR applications. These sensors measure the distance between the sensor and the encircling gadgets, supporting AR systems apprehend the layout and dimensions of the bodily environment. This statistics is used to properly align virtual items with real-world surfaces, ensuring that digital content is accurately located in the physical global. LiDAR is mainly beneficial in packages like architectural layout, navigation, and self sustaining vehicles, where precise spatial information is essential.

3. Cameras: Cameras are broadly used in each VR and AR structures to seize visual facts from the consumer's environment. In AR, cameras are used to recognize bodily items and places, allowing virtual factors to be overlaid onto actual-global scenes. These cameras, while blended with laptop vision algorithms, can carry out responsibilities consisting of

object popularity, face tracking, and surroundings mapping. In VR, cameras are frequently utilized in headset monitoring systems to discover the placement and orientation of the consumer's head and body.

4. Infrared Sensors: Infrared sensors are employed in both VR and AR packages to music the user's movements or discover objects inside a designated variety. These sensors are particularly beneficial in AR for gesture reputation and intensity sensing in environments with low visibility, as infrared mild can penetrate via boundaries like smoke or fog. In VR, infrared sensors in motion controllers can tune hand moves and gestures, making an allowance for greater herbal interactions inside virtual areas.

5. Pressure and Touch Sensors: Touch sensors, consisting of capacitive touchscreens or haptic comments gadgets, are vital in offering tactile comments throughout consumer interaction. These sensors allow VR and AR systems to locate touch, stress, or even the force applied by means of the person, contributing to a greater immersive experience. In VR, this comments can simulate the sensation of conserving items or interacting with environments. In AR, contact sensors can allow gesture-based control, allowing users to govern virtual gadgets with their hands.

While sensor technology seize great amounts of statistics from the bodily surroundings, data analytics equipment are essential to procedure and make sense of this information. By studying sensor statistics in actual-time, superior algorithms can adapt digital and augmented experiences to the consumer's behavior, choices, and surroundings. The position of facts analytics is essential in improving each the realism and personalization of VR and AR stories.

In both VR and AR, actual-time facts processing is vital for developing a responsive and dynamic experience. For example, in VR, the system have to continuously examine motion sensor facts to update the person's function within the digital environment. Any put off in processing this records can cause motion sickness or disorientation. Similarly, in AR, real-time information analytics permits for accurate item recognition and interplay, ensuring that virtual elements remain aligned with the physical world because the consumer moves or modifications their point of view.

One of the important thing benefits of integrating data analytics with sensor technologies is the capability to personalize the person enjoy. By amassing and analyzing facts on consumer interactions, possibilities, and behavior, VR and AR systems can adapt in real time, providing a tailored revel in. For instance, in VR gaming, analytics can track a participant's overall performance, adjusting problem degrees primarily based on their ability and development. In AR, data analytics can offer context-aware content, which include location-primarily based information or customized tips based at the user's environment.

Machine gaining knowledge of and synthetic intelligence (AI) play an vital function inside the facts analytics manner. These technology enable structures to no longer simplest system statistics however also analyze from it over time. By utilizing AI algorithms, VR and AR systems can constantly improve the pleasant of reports, making them greater intuitive and accurate. For instance, AI fashions can expect person behavior based totally on previous interactions, adjusting the digital surroundings or the way virtual objects are displayed consequently.

Predictive analytics, driven by way of gadget studying and AI, is remodeling the way VR and AR systems reply to users. By studying historical statistics and user tendencies, predictive models can forecast destiny actions or needs. In VR and AR, this may cause systems that expect what a consumer would possibly do next, adjusting the digital environment proactively to enhance immersion.

For example, in schooling simulations, predictive analytics can anticipate how a user is probably to react to certain situations, adjusting the scenario in real time. This guarantees that the schooling enjoy stays tough and attractive. Similarly, in AR programs, predictive analytics can provide customized content based on person behaviors, environmental elements, and contextual facts, enhancing the overall person enjoy.

The combination of sensor technologies and statistics analytics has some distance-reaching applications throughout industries, starting from healthcare to entertainment and manufacturing.

1. Healthcare: In healthcare, VR and AR applications are using sensor records and analytics to enhance clinical education, affected person care, and rehabilitation. Sensors can tune a affected person's physical actions, providing actual-time comments on their progress throughout bodily remedy. In scientific simulations, VR and AR structures use real-time records to create sensible training environments for medical specialists, letting them exercise tactics effectively and effectively.

2. Manufacturing and Industry: In business settings, sensors and records analytics are essential for predictive renovation, education, and best manipulate. AR systems use sensors to offer employees with real-time data about machinery, assisting them to become aware of capability issues earlier than they reason screw ups. Data analytics allows optimize workflows, decreasing downtime and growing efficiency in manufacturing environments.

3. Entertainment and Gaming: In enjoyment, VR gaming platforms rely upon sensors to create immersive studies, allowing players to have interaction with digital worlds the usage of movement tracking, hand gestures, and haptic comments. Data analytics performs a function in tailoring

gameplay experiences, adjusting eventualities primarily based on participant possibilities and talent degrees.

4. Education: Sensor technologies and facts analytics are revolutionizing schooling by way of creating interactive and immersive getting to know environments. VR structures can song a student's movements and reactions, adapting the gaining knowledge of fabric based totally on their progress. In AR, sensor statistics facilitates contextualize instructional content material, providing students with personalized and area-based learning stories.

Despite the splendid ability of sensor technologies and information analytics in VR and AR, there are several demanding situations that ought to be addressed. Sensor accuracy, latency, and power intake are some of the technical hurdles that want improvement to make certain seamless experiences. Moreover, the large quantities of records generated with the aid of sensors ought to be efficaciously processed and stored, which raises concerns about information privacy and safety.

As sensor technologies and facts analytics retain to adapt, the future of VR and AR may be fashioned by using improvements in those areas. Advances in AI and machine studying will allow even extra customized and adaptive reports, whilst upgrades in sensor accuracy and miniaturization will result in more intuitive and user-pleasant systems. The persisted improvement of real-time analytics and predictive modeling will make digital and augmented environments greater intelligent, interactive, and tasty than ever before.

8.3. Holography and 3D Imaging

Holography and 3-D imaging technologies have made giant advancements in recent years, using the development of greater immersive digital and augmented fact reports. These technologies provide the ability to seize, display, and have interaction with objects and environments in a way that carefully mirrors truth, offering a sense of intensity and dimensionality that traditional 2D imaging can't acquire. By allowing users to look and control 3-dimensional gadgets in real time, holography and 3D imaging are poised to revolutionize fields starting from enjoyment and healthcare to schooling and manufacturing.

Holography is a way that lets in the recording and reconstruction of mild patterns, creating a 3-dimensional representation of an object. Unlike traditional images, which captures a -dimensional picture, holography records the light's depth and the phase records, allowing the reconstruction of the object's 3D form, texture, and depth. When regarded, holograms may be discovered from distinct angles, supplying the illusion of a actual 3-d item.

The method of creating a hologram entails shining a laser onto the object being imaged. The light displays off the object and interacts with a reference beam, developing an interference pattern that is recorded onto a unique photographic plate or virtual sensor. When illuminated by means of the same light source, this interference pattern recreates the unique light waves, permitting the 3-d picture to be visible in full depth. Modern improvements in virtual holography, wherein the information is captured and processed by using computers, have improved the precision and resolution of holographic photographs.

Applications of Holography

1. Entertainment and Gaming: In leisure, holography is paving the way for extra life like and interactive reviews. Holographic projections can create interactive 3-d characters and environments that customers can interact with from exceptional perspectives, making the experience more immersive than conventional 2D screens or even some types of VR. In gaming, this allows players to interact with real-time holographic avatars and items, increasing the sense of presence in virtual worlds.

2. Medical Imaging: One of the maximum promising packages of holography is within the field of healthcare, in which 3D holographic imaging is being used for scientific visualization. For example, holographic shows of organs and tissues permit doctors and surgeons to have a look at complicated structures in greater element, improving diagnosis and surgical making plans. Surgeons also can use holographic visualizations to exercise and plan approaches on 3-D

representations of patient anatomy, doubtlessly enhancing effects and lowering the dangers of surgical treatment.

3. Telecommunication: Holography is also revolutionizing conversation, especially inside the realm of faraway collaboration. By developing lifestyles-sized 3-D holograms of humans and objects, it's miles feasible to preserve greater realistic virtual meetings and interactions, presenting a stage of presence and engagement that is not feasible with conventional video conferencing. Holographic telepresence allows humans to have interaction in a extra natural and dynamic manner, mimicking in-individual conferences at the same time as removing geographical barriers.

4. Art and Design: Artists and designers are starting to incorporate holography into their innovative procedures, the use of it to show off their works in new and modern approaches. For example, holographic projections can create digital artwork installations, permitting visitors to revel in sculptures and artwork from all angles with out the want for bodily gadgets. This opens up new opportunities for creating interactive and evolving art forms that reply to the presence and actions of the viewer.

3D imaging, on the other hand, entails shooting real-global items and environments as 3-dimensional models or pictures. Unlike conventional 2D images, which most effective captures the peak and width of an object, 3-D imaging technologies upload depth to create a greater realistic and complete representation of the physical world. Several techniques and gear are used in 3D imaging, together with stereo vision, LiDAR scanning, and photogrammetry.

1. Stereo Vision: Stereo vision is a method that makes use of or greater cameras to seize pictures from unique angles. By evaluating these photographs, intensity records can be inferred, permitting the creation of 3D fashions of the scene or object. This method is broadly utilized in packages like robotics, self sufficient automobiles, and augmented reality, where knowledge the depth and spatial relationships among gadgets is critical.

2. LiDAR (Light Detection and Ranging): LiDAR is a faraway sensing technique that makes use of laser pulses to degree distances and create quite accurate 3-D representations of environments. By measuring the time it takes for laser pulses to go back after hitting an object, LiDAR can generate particular 3-D maps with excessive resolution. LiDAR is specifically useful in packages including independent navigation, mapping, and 3D scanning of landscapes or homes.

3. Photogrammetry: Photogrammetry includes using snap shots taken from multiple angles to create a 3D version of an item or scene. This technique is regularly utilized in archaeology, architecture, and virtual historical past renovation to create accurate 3-d representations of real-international objects or environments. By analyzing the images, software can

extract intensity facts and generate a textured 3-D version that can be explored surely.

Applications of 3-D Imaging

1. Virtual and Augmented Reality: 3-D imaging performs a key role in VR and AR applications, permitting virtual gadgets to be integrated into actual-global environments. In AR, 3-D imaging permits the introduction of virtual items that seem to engage with the real international in real time. For example, virtual fixtures can be positioned within a user's living room, and the 3-D model will correctly replicate the dimensions and perspectives of the physical space. In VR, 3D fashions create extra immersive and interactive studies, in which users can control and discover virtual items from all angles.

2. Healthcare: In addition to holography, 3-D imaging is likewise making big strides in clinical applications. 3-d scans of organs, tissues, or even character cells permit healthcare professionals to advantage deeper insights into the human body, improving analysis, treatment making plans, and surgical precision. Medical imaging techniques like MRI, CT scans, and ultrasound are increasingly getting used to generate 3-d models of patients, offering extra targeted and accurate statistics for doctors and surgeons.

3. Manufacturing and Product Design: In industries such as production and product design, 3D imaging is used to create correct fashions of prototypes and components, permitting designers and engineers to simulate overall performance,

perceive capability problems, and refine designs before production. This process, called 3-D prototyping or fast prototyping, quickens the design cycle and improves product high-quality by means of catching design flaws early.

4. Cultural Heritage and Preservation: 3-D imaging is likewise getting used to hold and digitally archive cultural background sites, artifacts, and historic gadgets. Through the introduction of 3-D fashions, archaeologists, curators, and historians can have a look at and share these items with out physically handling them, stopping harm and making sure their long-time period protection. Additionally, 3D imaging permits the endeavor of historic web sites that can be liable to destruction because of natural or human-made causes.

As the skills of holography and 3-D imaging preserve to enhance, the ability programs of those technology will extend dramatically. Advances in computational strength, sensor accuracy, and information processing will permit for the creation of extra sensible and detailed holograms and 3-D fashions. Furthermore, the combination of artificial intelligence and machine getting to know will beautify the ability to generate, manage, and engage with 3D statistics in real time.

The destiny of holography and 3-d imaging holds exciting possibilities, inclusive of the creation of absolutely immersive, interactive holographic shows that customers can have interaction with directly. This may want to revolutionize industries which include enjoyment, education, healthcare, and even retail, in which customers should revel in services and products in 3-d earlier than making purchasing selections.

As holography and 3D imaging technologies preserve to adapt, they will blur the strains between the bodily and digital worlds, permitting richer, greater sensible experiences and developing new opportunities for innovation across diverse sectors.

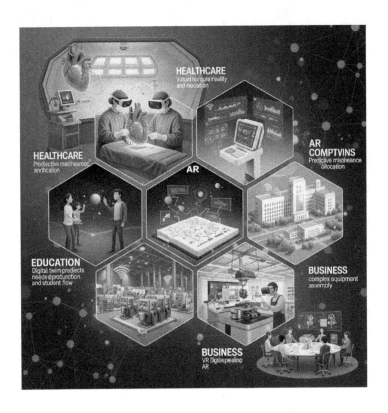

CHAPTER 9

Current and Future Applications of Digital Twins

9.1. Applications in Health and Medicine

Digital twins, the virtual replicas of bodily entities or systems, have discovered transformative applications in diverse sectors, which includes fitness and medication. Their capacity to simulate actual-time statistics from the bodily global and generate predictive models has the potential to revolutionize healthcare by improving diagnostics, remedy planning, patient care, and operational efficiency within medical establishments. Digital twins in healthcare aren't only a concept; they are increasingly more getting used to enhance precision, reduce prices, and improve affected person outcomes. The key areas of utility in health and medicine encompass personalised healthcare, scientific device optimization, surgical making plans, and public health.

One of the most promising programs of digital twins in healthcare is personalised medicine. By growing a virtual twin of a affected person, medical experts can simulate the individual's physiology and expect how their body will reply to diverse remedies. These virtual replicas are created by using integrating statistics from multiple assets, which includes clinical imaging, genetic profiles, wearables, and digital health facts. Through the usage of synthetic intelligence and system mastering, the digital dual can evolve in actual time to reflect the affected person's modern health fame and are expecting ability health dangers.

For example, a digital dual of a patient's coronary heart can be advanced primarily based on facts from echocardiograms, MRI scans, and different diagnostic gear. This model should then be used to expect how the coronary heart would respond to a brand new remedy or remedy, allowing doctors to select the handiest therapeutic option tailored to that patient's specific condition. This manner not most effective facilitates in choosing the right treatment but also minimizes the trial-and-error method historically associated with many scientific therapies, specifically in complicated sicknesses like most cancers, cardiovascular illnesses, and diabetes.

Digital twins are also getting used to optimize the design, overall performance, and upkeep of clinical devices. For instance, virtual twins can simulate the behavior of scientific device together with pacemakers, insulin pumps, or prosthetics, helping engineers and clinicians recognize how these gadgets characteristic in real-life situations. By jogging simulations and analyzing the device's performance in numerous environments, manufacturers can enhance tool reliability and reduce the likelihood of failure.

In the case of implantable devices, digital twins can also be used to music and display the lengthy-term overall performance of the tool in the human frame. For instance, a virtual twin of a prosthetic limb can offer insights into the wear and tear of the tool and expect when it could need servicing or substitute, helping to extend the life of the tool and ensuring patient protection.

Digital twins are revolutionizing surgical planning and training via allowing surgeons to rehearse and refine their techniques on fantastically correct, patient-specific models. Before performing a process, surgeons can create a virtual twin of the affected person's anatomy primarily based on 3-D scans and medical imaging statistics, permitting them to plot the surgery with excessive precision. This functionality is especially essential for complex surgeries in which information of tricky anatomical systems is important.

For instance, in spinal surgical procedures, where minute adjustments can notably impact affected person outcomes, digital twins can offer surgeons with a virtual model of the backbone, permitting them to simulate special surgical tactics and perceive the first-rate course before making an incision. Similarly, in neurosurgery, virtual twins may be used to map out the brain's intricate community of blood vessels, nerves, and tissues, allowing surgeons to avoid essential regions all through surgical operation.

Additionally, virtual twins may be employed for surgical schooling and simulation. By creating incredibly exact, interactive fashions of human anatomy, surgical trainees can practice methods in a digital environment before acting them on real sufferers. This not most effective enhances talent acquisition but additionally reduces the danger of human error in the course of actual surgeries.

A key aspect of virtual twins in healthcare is their potential to provide non-stop, actual-time tracking of patients' fitness. Wearables and other scientific devices can acquire significant amounts of statistics, including heart rate, blood strain, oxygen levels, and different critical signs and symptoms. This facts is then fed into the affected person's virtual dual, that could constantly replace its version to reflect the patient's modern fitness fame.

By studying this records, virtual twins can hit upon early symptoms of degradation or headaches in a patient's situation. For instance, a virtual twin of a diabetic affected person can monitor their glucose tiers and expect whilst insulin changes is probably necessary. Similarly, inside the case of continual situations like bronchial asthma, the virtual dual can offer signals if environmental factors or modifications in lung function are possibly to cause an attack.

Furthermore, virtual twins can be included with AI-pushed predictive algorithms which can forecast capacity medical events, which includes heart assaults or strokes, by way of studying trends inside the affected person's health facts. Early intervention primarily based on those predictions can improve results and reduce the want for emergency interventions.

Digital twins also are reworking the landscape of drug improvement and scientific trials. Traditionally, scientific trials are a prolonged and steeply-priced technique, with many tablets failing to attain the marketplace due to unexpected facet consequences or lack of efficacy. By growing digital twins of patients, pharmaceutical businesses can behavior simulations of how exclusive populations may reply to a brand new drug with out the want for large-scale human trials.

These digital models permit researchers to simulate drug interactions, aspect consequences, and most fulfilling dosing in a managed and chance-loose environment. The end result is quicker drug development cycles and greater correct predictions of a drug's effectiveness in the actual international. Digital twins can also reduce the want for animal checking out, offering a more moral and efficient technique to preclinical research.

Digital twins aren't restrained to individual affected person care; additionally they have great programs in public fitness. By growing virtual twins of whole populations or towns, health corporations can are expecting and manipulate sickness outbreaks, optimize healthcare resource allocation, and enhance public fitness planning. For instance, throughout a virus, digital twins can simulate the spread of disease within a populace, supporting to predict hotspots and tell quarantine or vaccination efforts.

Moreover, virtual twins can help healthcare structures optimize sanatorium workflows, manage bed occupancy, and enhance the shipping of services. By simulating affected person flow, team of workers availability, and resource utilization, hospitals can enhance their operational efficiency and provide higher care to extra patients.

The future of digital twins in healthcare holds extremely good capability. As era continues to adapt, virtual twins turns into even greater correct, targeted, and incorporated with different rising technology together with synthetic intelligence, gadget studying, and blockchain. With the combination of AI, virtual twins might be capable of predict and optimize treatment plans greater effectively, while real-time information evaluation will allow for more personalized, information-driven selection-making.

The destiny also includes using virtual twins to control complex, multi-disciplinary care groups. By permitting seamless collaboration amongst experts, digital twins can facilitate coordinated take care of sufferers with complicated situations. As digital twins turn out to be extra good sized, they may play a relevant function in stopping sicknesses, imparting real-time remedy adjustments, and improving ordinary healthcare efficiency.

As healthcare systems keep to move toward extra affected person-centric and data-driven processes, virtual twins will be at the forefront of reworking the industry, paving the manner for a destiny where healthcare is greater predictive, personalised, and efficient.

9.2. Education and Learning Experiences

9.2.1. Virtual Reality and Augmented Reality in Education

Virtual Reality (VR) and Augmented Reality (AR) have added profound adjustments to the instructional landscape, supplying immersive, interactive, and tasty gaining knowledge of studies which are reshaping how training is brought and experienced. These technologies are pushing the bounds of traditional school rooms and permitting new styles of studying, enhancing both coaching techniques and pupil engagement.

One of the maximum great blessings of VR and AR in training is the introduction of immersive getting to know environments that engage students in ways traditional techniques can't. In VR, students may be transported to totally distinct environments, allowing them to explore complex clinical concepts, ancient occasions, or geographical locations in 3-d area. For instance, VR simulations can vicinity students at the surface of Mars, underwater in a coral reef, or within the human frame to have a look at biological processes in movement. This level of immersion fosters a deeper expertise of challenge remember and might considerably enhance retention charges, as students aren't merely passive beginners however energetic members inside the instructional revel in.

In assessment, AR enriches the real international with the aid of covering virtual content onto physical surroundings. By the usage of smartphones, tablets, or AR glasses, students can interact with digital objects that appear to exist in the actual world. This is mainly powerful in fields like anatomy, in which students can view and engage with 3-D fashions of organs and structures as if they were gift in the room. AR transforms conventional textbooks into dynamic, interactive gaining knowledge of gear, turning static diagrams into interactive models and helping to make abstract concepts greater tangible.

VR and AR provide new methods to help lively gaining knowledge of. In a traditional school room, college students frequently depend on textbooks or lectures to recognize theoretical principles, but VR and AR deliver those concepts to existence. For instance, in scientific training, college students can use VR to practice surgical methods in a digital environment, gaining practical experience without the threat associated with practising on real sufferers. Similarly, engineering college students can use VR to simulate designing and building structures, interacting with virtual models of bridges, homes, or equipment to check and enhance their designs.

AR packages additionally guide lively getting to know by presenting interactive equipment that assist students control statistics or standards in actual-time. For instance, a chemistry pupil should use AR to visualize molecular structures in 3-D, enabling a deeper expertise of chemical reactions and atomic interactions. This type of interactive mastering encourages hassle-solving and important wondering, abilties that are critical for achievement in the present day global.

VR and AR technologies play a good sized role in making education greater accessible and inclusive for students with disabilities. For college students with bodily disabilities, VR can offer simulations of stories they could in any other case not have get entry to to, consisting of area journeys or hands-on labs. For instance, students with mobility impairments can be able to take a virtual tour of a museum or go to a far off region, permitting them to take part in activities that might be challenging in the physical international.

Additionally, AR can help students with gaining knowledge of disabilities. By presenting actual-time translations, voice reputation, and textual content-to-speech functionality, AR apps can help students with analyzing or comprehension problems. These technology smash down conventional barriers to studying, ensuring that education is extra equitable and adaptable to the needs of numerous student populations.

One of the most effective consequences of VR and AR is their capability to enhance pupil engagement. Traditional educational techniques often warfare to preserve students' interest, however VR and AR offer immersive, interactive reports which can be inherently enticing. These technology enchantment to college students' natural curiosity and love of exploration, motivating them to take part greater actively in their studying.

In a VR history lesson, as an instance, college students can be transported again in time to witness considerable historic occasions firsthand, together with the signing of the Declaration of Independence or the development of the Great Wall of China. By interacting with historical figures and exploring genuine, 3D-rendered environments, students advantage a experience of connection to the situation rely that makes studying extra exciting and noteworthy.

In addition to engagement, VR and AR also can foster collaboration and teamwork. Many VR environments allow more than one college students to have interaction with each other in actual-time, creating opportunities for organization trouble-solving, shared reviews, and collaborative gaining knowledge of. In an AR-primarily based school room, students can paintings together to complete tasks, fixing demanding situations that require them to paintings in sync, improving their teamwork and communique capabilities.

In the context of distance studying and far off training, VR and AR are transforming the way college students participate in lessons. With VR, far off newbies can attend digital classrooms, where they could have interaction with instructors and classmates in a digital space that simulates the revel in of being bodily gift. This permits college students to have interaction in discussions, ask questions, and participate in activities that might historically require bodily presence, fostering a experience of connection and decreasing the isolation often related to faraway gaining knowledge of.

AR, too, has made distance learning extra dynamic. By integrating AR into on line courses, educators can provide students with virtual gadgets, fashions, or diagrams to decorate their getting to know. For instance, a scholar in a faraway place could use AR to interact with a 3D version of the solar gadget, gaining a fingers-on knowledge of planetary movement, or use AR apps to behavior technology experiments truly, making distance schooling more interactive and attractive.

Another region in which VR and AR are making an effect is in the realm of tests. Traditional trying out methods, consisting of written checks, often fail to degree students' capability to use know-how in real-world contexts. VR and AR offer new ways to assess college students thru simulations and interactive tasks. For example, in scientific education, VR can simulate a scientific environment wherein college students diagnose and treat virtual sufferers, offering a extra complete evaluation in their talents than a paper test ever could.

Additionally, those technology allow for actual-time comments. In VR-primarily based education eventualities, students may be given immediately corrective comments on their actions, allowing them to examine from their mistakes and adjust their strategies as needed. This immediate remarks loop facilitates college students analyze extra effectively and encourages non-stop improvement, a essential issue of the studying procedure.

Looking in advance, VR and AR are predicted to hold evolving and play a fair larger function in schooling. As the era turns into extra cheap and large, colleges and universities will in all likelihood undertake VR and AR on a bigger scale, making immersive learning stories reachable to students worldwide. With advancements in hardware, which include lighter headsets and greater powerful computing competencies, these technology turns into greater person-pleasant and broadly incorporated into curricula across loads of disciplines.

The mixture of VR, AR, and different emerging technology, which include AI and 5G, will also create new opportunities for customized and adaptive studying. For instance, AI algorithms can tune a student's development inside a VR or AR surroundings and alter the level of difficulty based totally on their man or woman needs and capabilities. This personalised method will make training extra tailor-made and powerful, catering to the precise learning kinds of every scholar.

VR and AR have the capacity to reshape the destiny of schooling, creating a extra immersive, reachable, and engaging studying enjoy that prepares college students for success in a swiftly evolving international. By allowing arms-on studying, improving engagement, and breaking down barriers to access, these technology will hold to convert how students examine, collaborate, and interact with the sector around them.

9.2.2. Advances in Digital Twins in the Healthcare Sector

The healthcare quarter has witnessed superb improvements in the application of Digital Twins (DT) generation, marking a transformative shift in how healthcare services are introduced, controlled, and optimized. The idea of Digital Twins in healthcare refers to the advent of digital models that reflect person sufferers' organic processes, imparting healthcare specialists with an advanced, real-time representation of a patient's health status. These digital fashions no longer most effective enhance patient care however also contribute appreciably to medical studies, scientific decision-making, and the layout of personalized treatment plans.

One of the most groundbreaking applications of Digital Twins in healthcare is the improvement of personalised remedy. By developing a Digital Twin of a patient, healthcare vendors can simulate various remedy alternatives and are expecting how the patient's body will reply to exceptional interventions. This allows docs to tailor treatment plans specially to the person, optimizing treatments primarily based at the affected person's specific genetic makeup, scientific records, and physiological characteristics.

For example, in oncology, medical doctors can create a Digital Twin of a most cancers affected person and simulate how one-of-a-kind chemotherapy regimens might have an effect on the tumor. This predictive modeling can help discover the most effective treatment plan earlier than it's far definitely administered, decreasing the risk of trial-and-error strategies which could lead to needless facet effects or delays in remedy. By the usage of a Digital Twin, the healthcare team can adjust the dosage or remedy approach in actual-time, improving the overall efficacy and minimizing unfavorable outcomes.

Digital Twins can also play a crucial function in preventative healthcare via enabling the prediction of future health troubles. By continuously collecting and reading records from wearable gadgets, sensors, and different health tracking equipment, a affected person's Digital Twin can be kept updated with actual-time data about their health popularity. This steady float of information permits healthcare vendors to tune capability health risks, along with the development of persistent situations like coronary heart disorder, diabetes, or high blood pressure, and interfere earlier than they strengthen into more critical issues.

For example, in cardiovascular health, a Digital Twin may be used to track adjustments in blood strain, heart price, and different vital parameters, presenting early warnings of potential cardiovascular events like coronary heart assaults or strokes. If the Digital Twin shows a regarding trend, healthcare vendors can proactively adjust the patient's care plan, which includes recommending life-style modifications, prescribing remedy, or appearing extra diagnostic tests to save you greater severe consequences.

Digital Twins are an increasing number of getting used inside the making plans and simulation of complex surgeries. By developing a digital model of a patient's anatomy, surgeons can simulate the process in a incredibly unique, practical surroundings, making sure that the operation is achieved as precisely as viable. This virtual rehearsal allows surgeons to pick out potential challenges or dangers earlier than entering the operating room, improving affected person effects and reducing the likelihood of headaches.

For example, in orthopedic surgery, Digital Twins can model the patient's skeletal structure and simulate the position of implants or prosthetics, ensuring that the process is optimized for the affected person's specific anatomical features. By visualizing and refining the surgical method inside the virtual international, surgeons can growth their self belief in appearing the method and decrease the possibilities of mistakes.

For sufferers with chronic diseases, Digital Twins offer the possibility for continuous tracking and control. Instead of relying on periodic visits to the medical doctor, a affected person's Digital Twin can be constantly updated with records from wearable gadgets, including heart fee monitors, glucose trackers, and hobby sensors. This permits healthcare vendors to continuously display a affected person's circumstance and interfere whilst necessary, frequently stopping exacerbations or complications from continual conditions.

For example, patients with diabetes could have their blood sugar stages monitored in actual-time, and their Digital Twin can tune fluctuations and provide signals while the tiers become dangerously excessive or low. This real-time feedback may be essential for dealing with persistent illnesses and making sure that patients keep top-quality health with out frequent clinic visits.

Digital Twins also are revolutionizing medical training and education. By using digital fashions of patients and medical scenarios, healthcare professionals can practice and hone their talents in a chance-unfastened, managed surroundings. These simulations can range from working towards diagnostic strategies to appearing complicated surgeries. Trainees can engage with the Digital Twin to discover diverse medical scenarios, study sickness development, and experiment with exclusive remedy options with out the risk of harming actual sufferers.

Medical students and citizens can use Digital Twins to discover affected person anatomy in 3-D, gaining a deeper knowledge of the human frame's shape and characteristic. This immersive learning revel in no longer most effective enhances their capabilities however additionally boosts their self assurance and preparedness when it comes to treating real patients.

The integration of actual-time tracking structures with Digital Twins is allowing medical doctors to make more knowledgeable selections during affected person care. In extensive care devices (ICUs), for instance, a patient's Digital Twin can continuously integrate facts from monitoring gadget together with coronary heart charge monitors, blood pressure cuffs, and oxygen sensors. This constant go with the flow of data allows healthcare providers to make well timed and properly-informed decisions, together with adjusting medications, changing ventilator settings, or altering the patient's treatment protocol based at the model's actual-time reaction.

The use of Digital Twins in real-time choice-making additionally complements the performance of healthcare shipping, because it reduces the time spent on facts evaluation and allows for quicker responses to adjustments in a affected person's situation.

The adoption of Digital Twins in healthcare holds the ability to improve patient effects and decrease average healthcare prices. By the usage of predictive analytics to count on fitness issues, customise remedy plans, and save you headaches, Digital Twins can reduce the need for steeply-priced interventions and health facility readmissions. Early detection of capability fitness issues can cause less luxurious treatments and save you sufferers from requiring emergency care or lengthy-time period hospitalization.

Furthermore, with the aid of optimizing surgeries, streamlining continual sickness control, and improving affected person monitoring, Digital Twins can growth the performance of healthcare transport, allowing vendors to allocate resources more successfully and offer care to extra patients with out compromising nice.

Advances in Digital Twin era in healthcare have ushered in a new era of precision medication, customized care, and proactive health management. As those technologies keep to evolve, their packages will only increase, leading to greater tailor-made, green, and powerful healthcare answers. The integration of Digital Twins into patient care has the ability to reshape the healthcare landscape, enhancing patient effects, decreasing prices, and improving the general experience for both healthcare companies and patients.

9.3. The Roles of Virtual Reality and Augmented Reality in the Business World

Virtual Reality (VR) and Augmented Reality (AR) are no longer simply emerging technologies; they have got become key drivers of innovation throughout various industries, transforming commercial enterprise operations, purchaser studies, and typical organizational techniques. As corporations try to live beforehand in a unexpectedly evolving digital panorama, the utility of VR and AR gives awesome blessings, revolutionizing sectors from marketing and retail to schooling and layout.

One of the most prominent makes use of of VR and AR in commercial enterprise is inside the enhancement of consumer enjoy. Both technology provide immersive, interactive environments that allow clients to interact with products and services in absolutely new ways. AR, mainly, offers companies the ability to overlay virtual facts onto the actual world. Retailers, as an example, use AR applications to help clients visualize merchandise in their personal homes earlier than making a purchase. Furniture shops, like IKEA, allow customers to location digital furnishings of their living areas via AR apps, presenting a sensible and interactive manner to choose merchandise.

VR, alternatively, gives a completely immersive enjoy, frequently used for virtual product demos, digital showrooms, or even digital journey studies. Luxury vehicle producers, as an example, use VR to present capacity consumers a totally immersive revel in in their automobiles, permitting them to customize the car's functions and take a look at drive it without a doubt with out leaving the showroom floor. Such experiences now not only beautify purchaser engagement however also foster a deeper connection among clients and types.

VR and AR are also an increasing number of used for education and simulation functions across industries. Businesses in sectors like manufacturing, healthcare, aviation, and navy schooling use VR to offer employees with immersive environments where they are able to learn and practice competencies with out the dangers related to actual-global situations. These technologies permit trainees to engage in practical simulations that reflect excessive-stakes situations, enabling them to advantage revel in and self assurance earlier than applying their abilities in actual operations.

In manufacturing, as an example, VR may be used to educate personnel on complex machinery or safety protocols with out the want for pricey bodily setups or the chance of accidents. Similarly, in healthcare, AR can help medical college students and experts in working towards surgical procedures or diagnostic techniques thru interactive 3-D models. These sorts of schooling equipment are becoming increasingly more sophisticated, taking into consideration more powerful and efficient getting to know.

The roles of VR and AR in product design and prototyping have revolutionized how companies method the improvement technique. Instead of depending completely on physical prototypes, which may be time-ingesting and highly-priced, companies now use VR and AR to create virtual prototypes that may be quickly modified and tested in virtual environments. This appreciably speeds up the layout system, enabling agencies to iterate on merchandise greater hastily and test a huge variety of designs earlier than committing to bodily manufacturing.

In automobile production, VR is regularly used for the design and trying out of motors. Engineers and architects can create virtual models of motors and take a look at how unique components interact or examine the ergonomics of the indoors earlier than a bodily prototype is built. This allows to shop both time and sources even as ensuring the product meets all layout requirements.

AR plays a complementary role in this technique by means of offering actual-time remarks to designers, displaying them how precise components or substances might behave whilst incorporated into the final product. For instance, using AR glasses, product designers can view and engage with virtual designs overlaid onto physical models, improving the accuracy and efficiency of the design manner.

VR and AR have come to be powerful equipment for advertising and marketing, allowing organizations to create enticing, interactive campaigns that seize the attention of their target audience. Rather than counting on conventional print or digital commercials, corporations are using immersive technologies to create memorable reviews that customers can engage with without delay.

For instance, AR is broadly utilized in advertising campaigns where purchasers can scan QR codes on packaging, commercials, or billboards to show extra data or engage in interactive content material. This might be some thing from viewing a 3-d version of a product to playing a branded recreation or receiving special offers. These interactive stories no longer most effective engage customers however also provide brands with precious information approximately consumer conduct and options.

VR, then again, is used to create immersive advertisements or reviews that take customers on a adventure. Brands like Coca-Cola and Adidas have included VR into their marketing techniques, growing immersive, branded stories that allow customers to engage with products or stories in a manner that conventional classified ads can't provide. These immersive marketing studies are exceedingly effective at growing logo take into account and purchaser engagement, main to more potent purchaser loyalty.

Another extensive software of VR and AR within the enterprise international is their position in enhancing far off collaboration and conversation. As corporations more and more embrace hybrid or fully far off paintings models, VR and AR provide gear that allow teams to collaborate and interact as though they were inside the identical physical vicinity. VR meetings, as an instance, permit remote employees to go into virtual meeting rooms, where they could engage with every other in a 3-D surroundings, imparting a experience of presence that video conferencing can't attain.

AR also can facilitate faraway work by using permitting personnel to overlay virtual data on their bodily surroundings. For example, a technician working remotely could use AR glasses to receive real-time guidance from a colleague, who could view the identical surroundings and provide step-by using-step instructions. This sort of support can enhance productiveness and decrease downtime, especially in fields that require technical understanding.

In deliver chain and logistics, AR and VR have tested to be valuable equipment for enhancing performance and accuracy. AR, as an example, is used to manual warehouse employees through the selecting and packing system with the aid of covering virtual commands and actual-time inventory facts onto their bodily surroundings. This no longer simplest will increase the velocity and accuracy of order success however also reduces the chance of mistakes, in the end improving customer pleasure.

VR, alternatively, is used for simulating logistics scenarios, allowing corporations to version deliver chain operations, take a look at unique eventualities, and optimize procedures before enforcing them inside the real global. This helps businesses become aware of capability bottlenecks or inefficiencies within the supply chain, allowing them to make statistics-pushed choices that enhance common overall performance.

The roles of Virtual Reality and Augmented Reality in the enterprise international are big and varied, encompassing a huge range of programs throughout industries. From enhancing patron stories and improving schooling strategies to revolutionizing product design and optimizing deliver chains, these technology are reshaping how agencies function and have interaction with their clients. As VR and AR preserve to adapt, their capability to drive innovation and create new business possibilities will most effective develop, positioning them as critical equipment inside the destiny of enterprise.

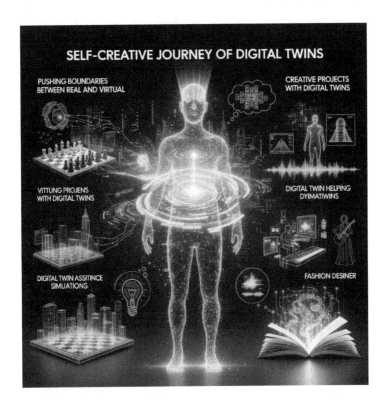

SELF-CREATIVE JOURNEY OF DIGITAL TWINS

PUSHING BOUNDARIES
BETWEEN REAL AND VIRTUAL

CREATIVE PROJECTS
WITH DIGITAL TWINS

VITTUNG PROJENS
WITH DIGITAL TWINS

DIGITAL TWIN HELPING
DYIMATIWINS

DIGITAL TWIN ASSITINCE
SIMULATIONS

FASHION DESINER

CHAPTER 10

Digital Twins' Self-Creative Journey: Advanced Tips and Inspirations

10.1. A Guide to Creating Your Own Virtual World

Creating a digital global is not only a technical endeavor; it is an art form that requires creativity, imagination, and a robust knowledge of both the tools to be had and the goals of the experience you intention to create. The upward thrust of virtual twins has unfolded new opportunities for growing rich, immersive environments that mimic the real international while imparting the flexibility and innovation of the virtual realm. This guide delves into the process of creating a virtual international, imparting each sensible suggestions and creative notion to convey your vision to existence.

Before diving into the technicalities of digital world creation, the first step is to define your vision and understand the purpose of the sector you desire to create. Are you designing a global for training and simulation, for amusement, or for educational functions? Is your intention to construct a fairly practical virtual twin of a physical environment, or is the intention greater summary, specializing in creativity and artistic expression?

Once you have got a clear cause, you may start to consider the precise capabilities your virtual world will have. For example, a digital twin for an city planning mission could need to correctly represent the bodily format and infrastructure of a town, even as a digital fact game may also prioritize engaging storylines, dynamic character interactions, and expansive open-global environments.

Creating a digital international entails selecting the ideal tools and structures that can help carry your ideas to life. There are several powerful equipment and systems available for world-constructing, and every comes with its personal set of strengths and features that match extraordinary needs.

For developing extraordinarily particular and sensible environments, structures inclusive of Unreal Engine and Unity are widely used, especially for digital dual packages. These sport engines offer advanced functions, inclusive of extremely good portraits rendering, physics simulations, and strong scripting talents, making them perfect for growing sensible and interactive worlds. Both Unity and Unreal Engine also aid digital fact (VR) and augmented reality (AR) development, allowing you to convey immersive stories to life.

For less difficult, extra summary virtual worlds or interactive simulations, structures like Second Life or Roblox offer a person-friendly surroundings wherein creators can build, design, and personalize their worlds without having tremendous programming know-how. These platforms permit for fast prototyping and community-pushed design, supplying a unique approach to global-constructing this is handy to a much broader audience.

A key aspect of digital world advent is designing the environment wherein users will interact. Whether your purpose is to replicate a real-global space or invent a very fictional landscape, the surroundings should be designed with functionality and aesthetics in thoughts. Start by way of outlining the key capabilities of the environment, which include geography, structure, lighting fixtures, and textures.

For a virtual twin, this indicates amassing data from the bodily international that can be appropriately translated into the virtual environment. This should involve the use of 3D scanning technologies, GIS (Geographic Information Systems), and other mapping equipment to make sure the virtual space is as accurate as viable.

For extra resourceful worlds, creativity plays a larger role. Consider the temper or feeling you need to awaken in the person. Are you designing a vibrant, futuristic city, a darkish, dystopian landscape, or a serene, herbal world? The design choices you're making in terms of colours, lighting fixtures, and spatial preparations will considerably impact the person experience.

Interactivity is some other crucial issue of virtual global design. Users must be able to engage with the surroundings, whether via movement, item manipulation, or interaction with characters. Scripting is crucial for making gadgets inside the world interactive. For instance, doorways may additionally open while a consumer processes, objects can be picked up and used, or characters may additionally provide talk or missions primarily based on user input.

The level of element you include into your virtual international will rely upon its cause and the available assets. For a virtual dual, mainly one used for functions like city making plans, engineering, or healthcare, high degrees of element are essential to appropriately replicate the real-world device. This may encompass elaborate models of buildings, roads, and infrastructure, as well as sensible textures and lighting fixtures consequences that decorate the sense of immersion.

In comparison, for a recreation or artistic global, the extent of detail can also range primarily based at the style and visible direction you need to pursue. Some video games and virtual worlds thrive on minimalist, stylized designs, even as others are seeking for to acquire photorealism. Balancing the visual complexity of the surroundings with the performance capabilities of the platform you are the usage of is a key consideration, as overly designated environments may additionally stress system sources, leading to lag or terrible consumer reviews.

One of the defining features of digital twins is the mixing of real-time data from the physical international. This is an critical step for any virtual international desiring to accurately reflect and interact with its real-international counterpart. Real-time records can come from sensors, IoT gadgets, or other sources that reveal the situations of the real environment.

For instance, a digital dual of a manufacturing unit may use actual-time statistics from sensors on the manufacturing unit floor to show stay updates about equipment, manufacturing levels, or environmental conditions. This facts can be displayed inside the virtual global to create a dynamic, responsive experience. In contrast, a gaming global or innovative space won't require real-time facts but could alternatively comprise other kinds of dynamic content, which include consumer-generated objects or procedurally generated environments that evolve over time.

Creating a virtual world is an iterative procedure that calls for constant testing and refinement. As you construct your global, frequently take a look at it for bugs, overall performance problems, and consumer experience. Are the interactions intuitive? Does the environment experience immersive? Are there any technical system faults that save you users from completely engaging with the sector?

User feedback is priceless at some stage in this level. Whether you're growing a virtual twin for a commercial enterprise cause or creating a recreation for entertainment, concerning others inside the testing system can provide sparkling insights and screen ability regions for development that might not be at once apparent.

Once your digital world is whole, it's time to proportion it with the sector. Depending for your goals, this can mean launching it for public access or proscribing get admission to to unique users. Digital twins frequently contain controlled get entry to to proprietary or personal information, whilst games and amusement worlds are typically designed for broader consumption.

For worlds which might be to be shared with a huge target audience, remember platform distribution techniques including sport stores (for VR games), net-primarily based platforms, or corporate servers (for enterprise-orientated digital twins). Sharing your international with the right audience is critical for attaining your favored effect, whether or not it's presenting precious facts insights or unique users with a totally immersive revel in.

Creating a digital global is an thrilling, multifaceted system that blends creativity, generation, and purpose. By virtually defining your desires, selecting the right tools, and designing an immersive, interactive enjoy, you can craft a digital global that now not only seems and feels actual but additionally provides meaningful engagement for users. Whether your undertaking is a digital dual of the actual international, a dynamic game, or an interactive instructional device, the opportunities for what you may create are restricted most effective through your imagination. The key to success lies in an ongoing commitment to innovation, iteration, and a deep information of both the technical and innovative components of virtual international-building.

10.2. Pushing the Boundaries Between the Real World and the Virtual World

The convergence of the actual international and the virtual world is one of the most groundbreaking traits in modern-day technology. The continuous blurring of those barriers, through technology along with virtual twins, virtual reality (VR), and augmented fact (AR), is remodeling industries, stories, and our notion of fact itself. The capacity to create immersive, interactive, and fairly designated virtual environments that engage seamlessly with the actual world opens up a realm of opportunities that had been as soon as limited to technology fiction.

The idea of merging the physical and virtual worlds isn't always new. Early virtual fact structures sought to create completely immersive environments where users could revel in a computer-generated global as though it had been actual. However, the modern generation of virtual technology, such as AR, VR, and digital twins, has taken this idea lots further through integrating actual-time statistics, allowing digital environments to respond to changes in the real world instantly.

One of the most vast steps in this direction is the improvement of digital twins, which can be digital replicas of real-international objects, systems, or environments. Digital twins not most effective reflect the physical international however also can have interaction with it. These digital replicas are continuously up to date with records from sensors and other assets, allowing actual-time synchronization between the bodily and virtual worlds. This dynamic interplay permits organizations, towns, or even complete industries to display, examine, and optimize methods remotely.

For instance, inside the field of city making plans, digital twins of cities allow planners and choice-makers to simulate numerous scenarios based on real-time statistics, consisting of site visitors patterns, electricity utilization, or environmental changes. This now not simplest enables in planning for the future but also aids in making knowledgeable selections to enhance sustainability, performance, and safety. By integrating the actual-time overall performance of bodily assets with digital fashions, these structures allow groups to check, modify, and optimize tactics with out risking physical assets.

Virtual reality has additionally end up a effective tool for immersing users in experiences that stretch the limits of the bodily global. Through the usage of VR headsets and specialised equipment, customers can explore new environments, take part in simulations, and interact with virtual items as though they were physically gift. These environments are regularly designed to be so realistic that customers can forget about they are in a digital world. As VR era maintains to evolve, the line among the real and digital worlds becomes increasingly difficult to parent.

Moreover, augmented reality (AR) is gambling a sizable position in pushing the boundaries of interaction among the actual and digital nation-states. Unlike VR, which completely immerses customers in a virtual surroundings, AR overlays digital elements onto the real global. This allows customers to have interaction with both physical and digital gadgets concurrently, developing a more seamless mixing of the 2. AR is used in various industries, from retail (wherein clients can try on garments in reality) to remedy (wherein surgeons can overlay digital information in the course of methods). The potential to beautify actual-global environments with digital overlays adds a layer of functionality and interactivity that has the ability to revolutionize how we revel in ordinary life.

The future of those technologies lies of their potential to end up even greater incorporated. We are moving closer to a destiny wherein the virtual and bodily worlds are not separate domain names but interconnected structures that tell and affect one another. Advances in 5G networks, AI, and part computing will most effective decorate this convergence by allowing faster records processing and more sophisticated interactions between digital and bodily environments.

In the business international, this integration is already obvious in fields like far flung work, customer service, and education. Digital twins are enabling organizations to create virtual fashions of their operations and provide employees with faraway access to actual-time data and digital simulations. This permits workers to make choices based on up-to-date statistics, increasing productivity and reducing risks. For instance, producers are the usage of digital twins to monitor machinery performance and identify issues earlier than they turn out to be main troubles, minimizing downtime and upkeep prices.

The enjoyment enterprise is also pushing the boundaries by using integrating AR, VR, and combined truth (MR) into immersive stories. Theme parks, museums, and stay activities are using these technologies to create interactive experiences that convey digital elements into the real international, providing attendees with new methods to engage with the content material. The capacity for storytelling in VR and AR has grown exponentially, with creators now able to build worlds that respond to consumer alternatives in real-time, growing stories which can be dynamic and notably personalized.

As these technologies continue to strengthen, the query of how to manipulate the interaction among the real and virtual worlds turns into extra critical. The improvement of standards and moral frameworks will be necessary to make sure that the integration of those technology remains responsible and beneficial. Issues of privacy, security, and statistics safety will want to be addressed as extra private and touchy records is shared and processed in each virtual and physical spaces.

The ongoing fusion of the actual and digital worlds is transforming how we have interaction with generation, revel in environments, and technique hassle-fixing. By pushing the boundaries among these realms, digital twins, VR, and AR are permitting a new era of opportunities, from optimized commercial enterprise operations to greater human reviews. As we continue to improve these technology, we will anticipate even greater interesting trends so that it will blur the road between the physical and virtual worlds, developing a destiny wherein the 2 are seamlessly interconnected.

10.3. Creative Projects and Experiences with Digital Twins

The introduction of digital twins, coupled with advancements in virtual truth (VR) and augmented fact (AR), has opened up new possibilities for innovative expression. By merging the digital with the real, virtual twins have transformed how innovative initiatives are conceived, developed, and skilled. Artists, designers, and creators throughout industries are exploring the capacity of virtual twins to craft progressive digital experiences, pushing the bounds of what is feasible in both the physical and digital nation-states.

One of the maximum exciting aspects of virtual twins in creative initiatives is their ability to provide distinctly special, dynamic, and responsive virtual environments. In these environments, each detail of a real-world item, character, or space may be captured and replicated digitally. This lets in creators to build interactive reports that are not best visually charming but additionally deeply immersive, blurring the lines between the actual and virtual worlds. By utilising digital twin generation, creators can manipulate and reimagine their environments in approaches that were previously unattainable.

10.3.1. Encouraging Creativity in Virtual Reality Projects

The integration of digital twins with virtual reality has spread out a huge range of possibilities for innovative initiatives. VR's immersive nature lets in users to step into fully found out digital environments which might be built upon the information provided with the aid of virtual twins. For artists, architects, and architects, VR gives an possibility to visualise and interact with their creations in methods that conventional techniques cannot mirror. This degree of interplay encourages innovation, allowing creators to refine and experiment with their ideas in a simulated but particularly accurate digital international.

For instance, within the field of structure, digital twins can be used to create digital replicas of homes or complete city environments. These fashions can be manipulated in VR, allowing architects to discover different layout variations or to visualise how a constructing may appearance in its actual-international context. The use of VR no longer simplest gives a practical preview of architectural tasks however additionally offers a area for collaborative creativity. Designers can walk via their virtual buildings, adjusting elements in actual time and making selections based totally on an immersive enjoy that closely mimics the physical world.

Similarly, digital twins are being employed in the gaming industry to create immersive, interactive virtual worlds. Game builders are using digital twin generation to craft hyper-sensible virtual environments that mirror real-world settings. These environments respond dynamically to player actions, growing a rich and tasty enjoy. This level of realism in VR gaming permits gamers to have interaction with the virtual world in a greater natural way, making choices and exploring environments as although they have been bodily gift.

Artists and media creators are also tapping into the capability of digital twins to generate innovative studies. By using virtual twin models, creators can blend the boundaries among the bodily and digital worlds in new, notion-frightening approaches. The utility of virtual twins in art lets in for a fusion of conventional art bureaucracy with current technology, ensuing in digital installations that evolve in response to the viewer's presence or actions. These interactive installations regularly depend upon VR or AR to interact audiences, growing a deeper connection between the viewer and the paintings.

Digital twins also provide interesting possibilities for interactive storytelling. Filmmakers and recreation builders can create environments that evolve and exchange based totally on audience interplay. This creates greater customized, enticing narratives where the story is not static but responds to the picks made by using the viewer or player. Such stories can be carried out across distinct genres, from immersive documentaries to virtual theater performances.

The future of innovative tasks with virtual twins is surprisingly promising. As technology maintains to conform, virtual twins becomes more specific, interactive, and reachable to a much wider range of creators. With the integration of artificial intelligence (AI) and system mastering, virtual environments powered by using virtual twins will become even extra responsive and adaptive. Creators may be capable of design projects that not simplest mimic the actual international but count on and react to adjustments in real time.

Furthermore, the upward thrust of 5G networks and upgrades in cloud computing will permit for extra fluid, actual-time interactions with digital twins in virtual environments. This method that creators may be capable of collaborate remotely, sharing and editing virtual dual models in real time irrespective of their physical place. This international interconnectedness will foster move-disciplinary collaborations, allowing creators from unique fields—together with artwork, layout, structure, and technology—to work together in the introduction of groundbreaking virtual reviews.

Digital twins provide substantial capability for creative initiatives, allowing the development of modern and interactive experiences that push the boundaries of both the physical and virtual worlds. By leveraging the immersive strength of VR and AR, creators can produce tasks that not simplest mirror reality however additionally permit for dynamic interactions and experimentation. As digital dual generation keeps to evolve, it'll absolutely play a pivotal role in shaping the future of creative expression throughout industries.

10.3.2. Art and Content Creation with Digital Twins

The integration of virtual twins into the world of artwork and content advent represents a transformative shift in how artistic works are conceived, produced, and skilled. By mixing the precision of digital modeling with the creativity of human expression, virtual twins offer artists a brand new toolset to push the limits in their craft, developing art that isn't always most effective immersive but also interactive and dynamic.

One of the key features of virtual twins inside the context of art introduction is the ability to replicate actual-international items, environments, and phenomena within the virtual area with a excessive degree of constancy. This replication extends some distance past static representations, allowing for the advent of residing, evolving artwork that reacts to adjustments and interactions. Artists can use digital twins to model their physical works and manipulate them in a virtual space, creating new studies for viewers or individuals. This opens up an entirely new measurement for conventional art paperwork, such as sculpture and set up art, by means of allowing them to exist in both bodily and virtual forms simultaneously.

The digital art exhibition is one of the maximum big innovations delivered approximately via the aggregate of digital twins and virtual truth (VR). By developing virtual twins of physical artwork pieces, artists and curators can convey their exhibitions into digital areas, allowing audiences from all around the international to engage with the artworks in an immersive surroundings. This revel in is now not confined by means of physical location, as traffic can navigate the gallery, view pieces from distinct angles, and even interact with the art itself in a manner that might be not possible in a conventional setting.

For instance, a virtual dual of a sculpture can be manipulated in actual time, permitting the viewer to rotate, zoom, or even alternate factors of the work, imparting a deeper, greater personalized engagement. These digital dual artistic endeavors also can include interactive factors, wherein the viewer's movements or movements cause adjustments in the piece, developing an evolving dating between the observer and the artwork. This shift toward interactivity turns the audience from passive observers into active individuals, permitting them to form their experience and interpretation of the artwork.

Another exciting possibility that virtual twins present to artists is the capability to mixture the digital with the physical in new and progressive approaches. Traditional artwork bureaucracy like portray, sculpture, and images can now be reimagined with digital technology, ensuing in hybrid artistic endeavors that combine both physical and virtual elements. For example, a traditional painting may want to have an augmented truth (AR) overlay, where extra elements appear whilst considered through a telephone or AR glasses, growing a richer, layered enjoy. Digital twins can also be used to create interactive installations wherein the physical paintings responds to the viewer's moves, bridging the space between the real international and the digital realm.

In this manner, digital twins enable a fluid interplay among physical gadgets and their virtual opposite numbers. Artists can create content this is both grounded within the material global and infinitely extendable inside the virtual space, beginning up totally new avenues for inventive exploration. The fusion of physical and digital realities lets in for the creation of art which can exist simultaneously in multiple spaces and bureaucracy, expanding the idea of what art can be and wherein it can be experienced.

Beyond traditional excellent arts, digital twins also are revolutionizing content material creation in industries like movie, animation, and gaming. Filmmakers and animators are the use of digital twin era to create hyper-realistic 3-d models of real-global environments, characters, and objects. These fashions can then be manipulated inside digital environments to create scenes that blur the traces among fact and fiction. For instance, virtual twins of actual-international landscapes or cityscapes can be used as digital backdrops for films, taking into account surprisingly special, immersive settings that had been once not possible to recreate physically.

In the gaming enterprise, digital twins are hired to build sensible digital worlds. Game builders can use virtual twins to copy real-world places with great accuracy, imparting players the opportunity to explore acquainted environments in a very new, interactive way. Additionally, the actual-time adaptability of virtual twins way that those virtual worlds can alternate and evolve primarily based at the participant's actions, growing a dynamic, ever-changing enjoy.

The application of virtual twins in art and content advent encourages greater creativity and experimentation. Artists now not want to depend totally on conventional tools or mediums however can harness the power of virtual technology to explore new thoughts and strategies. Digital twins allow for speedy prototyping and new release, enabling creators to experiment with distinctive configurations and designs with out the constraints of bodily substances or processes. This speeds up the creative workflow, offering infinite opportunities for artists to push the limits of their craft.

Moreover, the mixing of AI and gadget gaining knowledge of with digital twins opens up in addition possibilities for innovation. By the usage of algorithms to analyze and control the virtual twin records, artists can generate new creative content material this is prompted by information styles or real-international variables. For example, an artist could create a digital dual of a natural panorama and use AI to simulate the consequences of weather trade, permitting them to explore the environmental effect in a visual and interactive way. This kind of information-pushed creativity is main to the emergence of latest varieties of art that not handiest assignment the conventional belief of what art is but additionally enhance critical questions on the function of era in shaping our understanding of the world.

As digital dual technology maintains to conform, its impact on the world of art and content material creation will handiest develop. The growing accuracy of digital twin modeling, coupled with improvements in virtual fact, augmented reality, and synthetic intelligence, will permit artists to create even greater complicated, interactive, and immersive works. In the future, art may additionally not be constrained to standard galleries or theaters but will exist throughout virtual structures, skilled in new and dynamic methods that go beyond bodily area.

Digital twins are not best reworking how we create and revel in art, but they may be also expanding the opportunities for content advent throughout diverse industries. Whether in traditional artwork paperwork, interactive installations, or virtual enjoyment, the mixing of digital twins into the creative technique is enabling the development of innovative, immersive reviews that undertaking the limits of art and technology.

CHAPTER 11

The Real-World Transformation of Digital Twins

11.1. The Societal Impact of Virtual Reality and Augmented Reality

The speedy evolution of virtual truth (VR) and augmented truth (AR) technologies has ushered in a profound transformation throughout more than one sides of society. These technologies have the capability to reshape how individuals have interaction with the world, how organizations function, and the way we experience truth itself. As virtual twins, virtual and augmented realities have converged, imparting novel approaches to version, simulate, and engage with actual-global environments, their societal impact is multifaceted and a ways-attaining.

One of the maximum big societal impacts of VR and AR is the shift in how individuals and communities perceive and enjoy the world around them. With the capability to immerse customers in absolutely virtual environments or overlay virtual content onto the bodily world, VR and AR can smash down geographical, cultural, and social obstacles, allowing humans to get entry to and interact with distant places, humans, and stories. This accelerated attain can foster greater empathy, knowledge, and connection among people from diverse backgrounds, growing possibilities for move-cultural trade and collaboration.

For example, VR has the ability to create fully immersive educational reviews, enabling college students to visit historical

260 | Can Bartu H.

landmarks, explore complex scientific concepts in interactive simulations, or engage with international friends in digital lecture rooms. Similarly, AR can decorate actual-global reports, supplying contextual statistics and interactive elements that decorate mastering, tourism, and enjoyment. In each cases, these technologies bridge the space between traditional getting to know environments and experiential, palms-on gaining knowledge of.

Moreover, VR and AR are riding innovation in industries like healthcare, in which they're getting used to improve medical training, decorate patient care, and assist in complicated surgeries. Surgeons can now practice complex methods in virtual environments, gaining precious enjoy without risk to patients. Similarly, patients can advantage from AR-assisted treatment plans that provide actual-time visualizations of their conditions or use VR as a therapeutic tool to help with ache control or intellectual health treatments.

The business international, too, has felt the ripple results of VR and AR technology. Companies are the use of those equipment for advertising, product layout, schooling, and customer support. Virtual showrooms, for example, allow customers to interact with merchandise in a totally digital area before making purchasing decisions. Augmented reality applications are also turning into critical in fields like manufacturing, wherein technicians can access real-time facts and instructions overlaid onto machinery, improving efficiency and lowering errors.

However, as with every transformative technology, the sizeable adoption of VR and AR comes with demanding situations. One significant subject is the impact on social interaction and mental properly-being. As humans increasingly more immerse themselves in digital worlds, there is growing concern about the potential for social isolation and the erosion of face-to-face communique abilties. Additionally, the lines among the virtual and physical worlds may also blur to such an extent that individuals battle to differentiate between the two, leading to issues of escapism, addiction, or detachment from truth.

Furthermore, VR and AR technology increase significant moral questions. The immersive and interactive nature of those technologies increases issues approximately data privateness, surveillance, and the ability for manipulation. As digital twins reflect the physical international in virtual environments, the information generated by means of those interactions could be used for functions that individuals won't fully recognize or consent to. This raises the need for robust ethical frameworks and regulations to make sure that VR and AR technologies are used responsibly and with respect for person privateness and autonomy.

Despite these challenges, the capacity for VR and AR to transform society is simple. As these technologies retain to evolve and mature, they will increasingly affect how we work, analyze, socialize, and understand the world around us. The integration of digital twins into these reviews further enhances the possibilities, creating new methods to engage with and understand complex systems in both the physical and virtual realms. The societal impact of VR, AR, and digital twins will undoubtedly be profound, shaping the future of human interplay, schooling, amusement, and past.

The societal effect of virtual and augmented reality technologies is both transformative and complicated. As those technology grow to be extra integrated into normal life, they may maintain to venture traditional standards of area, time, and reality. The opportunities for innovation, connection, and personal increase are tremendous, but so too are the challenges and moral concerns that ought to be addressed. As we pass ahead into an an increasing number of digital destiny, it is going to be essential to navigate these modifications thoughtfully and responsibly to make sure that VR, AR, and digital twins benefit society in meaningful and sustainable methods.

11.2. Transformation and the Future of the Business World

The integration of virtual truth (VR), augmented reality (AR), and digital twins into the enterprise world isn't only a passing fashion but a profound shift in how corporations function, innovate, and interact with clients. These technology are using the future of industries, changing commercial enterprise models, and creating new opportunities across various sectors. As VR, AR, and digital twins evolve, their effect on the commercial enterprise world is reshaping the whole lot from product development and advertising and marketing to customer service and personnel management.

One of the most full-size alterations is in the realm of product layout and development. Digital twins, which reflect actual-world assets in a virtual surroundings, permit companies to create particular simulations in their merchandise before bodily prototypes are even made. This permits agencies to check and refine designs in digital spaces, reducing prices, time, and resources that would in any other case be spent on physical checking out. For industries together with production, aerospace, and automotive, this ability to test with virtual prototypes in a threat-free digital area is revolutionizing the way merchandise are delivered to market.

Beyond product improvement, digital twins, VR, and AR are redefining client experiences. Companies are leveraging VR to create immersive, interactive buying experiences that permit customers to explore products in a 3-D digital environment. This is specifically useful for groups in industries like fashion, actual property, and furnishings, where customers can interact with products as though they were physically present. AR complements this revel in by overlaying virtual facts onto the physical world, permitting customers to visualise merchandise in their very own homes, try on garments really, or see how a chunk of furniture suits into their space.

In addition to enhancing the client journey, these technology are revolutionizing advertising strategies. With the immersive nature of VR and AR, brands can craft noticeably enticing and customized advertising and marketing campaigns that seize the attention of customers in new and modern methods. For instance, car organizations are using VR to provide virtual take a look at drives, permitting customers to experience their automobiles in a totally immersive virtual surroundings. Similarly, AR is being utilized in advertising and marketing to offer interactive and dynamic content material that draws customers in and engages them immediately with services or products.

The use of VR, AR, and virtual twins also has profound implications for worker training and body of workers development. In industries along with healthcare, aviation, and manufacturing, immersive VR simulations permit workers to practice complicated responsibilities and procedures in a chance-unfastened, controlled environment. Surgeons can rehearse surgeries in digital settings, and pilots can go through flight education with out moving into an actual cockpit. The capability to simulate excessive-stakes conditions without the want for physical assets or hazard makes education extra efficient, powerful, and accessible.

Moreover, these technologies are fostering a extra collaborative and far off work environment. VR platforms enable digital conferences in which employees from around the world can engage as if they have been within the identical room, sharing ideas and collaborating on tasks. With the global rise of faraway paintings, this form of digital collaboration is becoming more and more critical, permitting businesses to bridge geographical distances and keep productiveness notwithstanding bodily separation.

The destiny of the commercial enterprise world is likewise being formed by means of improvements in automation and artificial intelligence (AI), which can be turning into an increasing number of incorporated with VR, AR, and digital twins. AI-powered analytics are being used to process tremendous quantities of records generated through digital twins, imparting groups with insights which could pressure decision-making and improve operational performance. For instance, predictive protection powered with the aid of AI and virtual twins allows companies to anticipate gadget screw ups earlier than they occur, lowering downtime and optimizing aid utilization.

Looking beforehand, the capability for VR, AR, and virtual twins to similarly remodel the enterprise global is gigantic. As those technologies preserve to mature, they'll power greater personalization, permitting groups to tailor merchandise, offerings, and studies to individual clients on an remarkable scale. The use of virtual twins becomes even greater widespread, imparting organizations the capability to simulate complete ecosystems, from supply chains to production flooring, optimizing every facet of their operations.

However, along these improvements comes a need for organizations to address new demanding situations, in particular regarding records privacy, cybersecurity, and ethical issues. As corporations collect greater information thru VR, AR, and digital twins, safeguarding touchy information and making sure compliance with privateness guidelines turns into an increasing number of critical. Additionally, as the digital and bodily worlds merge, moral dilemmas around automation, activity displacement, and the digital divide must be cautiously taken into consideration and managed.

The transformation introduced about through VR, AR, and virtual twins is just the beginning of a bigger revolution in the enterprise global. These technologies aren't simplest enhancing how agencies design, marketplace, and sell merchandise however also are redefining how organizations operate internally, collaborate globally, and have interaction with customers. As those technology preserve to evolve, the commercial enterprise landscape turns into increasingly immersive, records-driven, and interconnected, imparting exceptional opportunities for innovation and growth. At the identical time, groups will want to navigate the moral, regulatory, and societal implications that accompany these powerful gear to make sure their accountable and sustainable use in the future.

11.3. The Convergence of Digital Twins with Art and Culture

The intersection of digital twins with art and subculture represents a groundbreaking evolution in how we experience, create, and hold artistic works. As digital truth (VR), augmented reality (AR), and digital twins preserve to mature, they are reshaping the creative and cultural landscapes by way of introducing new methods for creation, interplay, and maintenance. This convergence opens new avenues for artists, museums, and cultural institutions to engage with their audiences in ways that had been as soon as inconceivable.

Digital twins have already began to revolutionize the creation method in the world of artwork. Artists are using digital twin technology to create hyper-realistic virtual versions in their works earlier than they're physically constructed or displayed. For example, in sculpture and architecture, virtual twins offer a virtual prototype of a chunk, permitting artists to experiment with substances, shapes, and designs in a threat-loose virtual environment. This permits extra exploration and iterative development in approaches that have been no longer viable with conventional techniques, where the artist turned into confined by means of the physical nature in their medium.

The potential of digital twins extends past the creation of physical items; in addition they enable the exploration of digital nation-states of artistic expression. Artists are more and more the usage of VR to create immersive artwork reports that allow viewers to step interior their paintings, interacting with the surroundings and the materials in ways that have been once constrained to the creativeness. For example, an artist might layout a 3-d digital painting that the viewer can walk around or even manipulate, blurring the lines among the observer and the observed. This not best creates a wholly new creative language however also modifications the relationship among the artist and the target market, as viewers become lively participants inside the art instead of passive observers.

The position of virtual twins and VR within the cultural area extends past the creation of artwork to its preservation and presentation. Museums, galleries, and cultural establishments are increasingly using digital twins to keep valuable artifacts and ancient websites. By developing designated 3-d replicas of artifacts, sculptures, or even whole cultural background web sites, virtual twins provide a way to defend these treasures from degradation or destruction. In the occasion of a catastrophe or the ravages of time, these virtual twins function accurate, accessible facts of irreplaceable objects and places.

Moreover, virtual twins and VR are remodeling the manner audiences experience way of life. Virtual museums, where traffic can discover replicas of historic artifacts or stroll via recreated historical ruins from the consolation of their homes, are making cultural history extra handy to a international target market. This democratization of artwork and way of life breaks down geographical and economic limitations that once restricted get right of entry to to cultural experiences. Virtual tours of world-famend museums, archaeological websites, and ancient landmarks provide an immersive alternative to physical visits, even as nonetheless preserving the essence of the authentic works. For instance, a virtual twin of the Louvre or the Parthenon can provide virtual visitors the capability to discover those locations in detail, even if they're unable to journey there in man or woman.

Additionally, the convergence of virtual twins and culture is fostering new approaches for artists and audiences to have interaction with heritage. Interactive VR reports now allow customers to stroll thru recreated historical events, experiencing cultural memories in real time. For instance, a digital dual of historic Rome can allow a viewer to enjoy the city in its top, walking the streets, witnessing ancient moments, or interacting with characters from records. This brings history to existence in a manner that conventional media, like books or movies, can't. These immersive experiences can foster a deeper expertise and emotional connection to cultural history, making it more applicable and relatable to contemporary audiences.

Another interesting software is using virtual twins in the restoration of damaged artistic endeavors. Rather than depending totally on traditional strategies of conservation, professionals can create distinct 3-D scans of artworks to model and expect the results of aging, allowing them to make more knowledgeable choices approximately recovery efforts. In cases in which unique substances or info have been lost, these digital twins serve as a treasured reference point for reconstructing pieces to their authentic condition, all even as keeping the integrity of the piece. This fusion of generation and art preserves now not handiest the visible issue however also the emotional and historic significance of cultural artifacts.

Moreover, digital twins and AR are finding applications in interactive public art installations. These installations blend the actual world with virtual reports, allowing visitors to enjoy art that evolves primarily based on their physical presence or moves. For instance, a public artwork set up would possibly use AR to mission an art work that shifts and modifications based on where a person stands or how they have interaction with the piece. This makes the revel in of artwork more dynamic and personal, allowing anyone to create a unique interaction with the artwork.

While the opportunities provided by digital twins within the arts and subculture sectors are good sized, there are also important challenges to bear in mind. The ethics of digital replication, mainly when handling cultural historical past, is a subject of ongoing debate. The creation of digital twins of ancient artifacts and landmarks increases questions about authenticity, ownership, and cultural appropriation. How have to virtual replicas be dealt with, and who has the right to create or control them? As generation maintains to adapt, it is going to be vital to set up clean guidelines and ethical requirements to address those issues.

The dating between digital twins and artwork and subculture is in its early stages but holds monstrous potential. By combining the skills of virtual technology with the creativity of the human spirit, new types of artwork and cultural reviews are emerging that were previously unimaginable. This convergence now not best enhances the preservation and presentation of cultural treasures but also empowers artists to push the boundaries in their creativity, imparting clean and immersive methods to have interaction with audiences round the sector. As this space maintains to expand, the future of art and subculture will possibly be increasingly more intertwined with virtual generation, supplying new reports that increase our connection to the beyond, present, and destiny.

CHAPTER 12

Conclusions and Future Outlook

12.1. The Significance and Potential of Digital Twins

The idea of digital twins represents a transformative soar within the convergence of bodily and digital worlds. As technologies like virtual reality (VR), augmented truth (AR), and the Internet of Things (IoT) advance, virtual twins are becoming an increasing number of extensive across various sectors, with a profound effect on industries, agencies, and even people. The capability of virtual twins lies in their potential to duplicate and simulate actual-global gadgets, systems, and environments in virtual spaces, permitting unparalleled opportunities for innovation, performance, and hassle-fixing.

At its core, a digital dual is a virtual duplicate of a physical entity this is constantly up to date with actual-time facts, taking into consideration a detailed, dynamic illustration of the object, gadget, or technique it mirrors. This virtual model can be used for analysis, tracking, simulation, and optimization, offering a deep know-how of the conduct and performance of its real-global counterpart. The programs of digital twins are widespread, spanning throughout manufacturing, healthcare, city planning, strength, and amusement, among others.

In production, virtual twins are revolutionizing how products are designed, tested, and maintained. By developing a

276 | Can Bartu H.

virtual duplicate of an entire production line, as an example, producers can monitor performance, predict failures earlier than they take place, and optimize workflows to improve efficiency. The capability to simulate changes within the digital global earlier than enforcing them within the actual global considerably reduces risks and charges associated with product development and protection.

In healthcare, the capability of virtual twins is equally transformative. Through the introduction of personalised digital twins for sufferers, doctors can simulate treatments, are expecting the consequences of various clinical interventions, and offer more particular and tailor-made care. Digital twins in healthcare can also be instrumental in dealing with public health crises, as they permit for real-time tracking of healthcare infrastructure, the unfold of sicknesses, and useful resource allocation.

One of the maximum interesting factors of digital twins is their capability to drive the digital transformation of towns and concrete environments. Urban making plans and clever metropolis tasks are increasingly more utilizing virtual twins to version visitors flow, expect the impact of production initiatives, and optimize electricity utilization across urban infrastructures. By replicating entire towns or districts digitally, planners and policymakers can check specific scenarios and enhance decision-making, main to greater sustainable and efficient city spaces.

Furthermore, virtual twins are paving the manner for the advancement of the Internet of Things (IoT). The proliferation of connected devices generates a wealth of facts, a great deal of which can be harnessed to create extra correct and purposeful virtual twins. These gadgets, whether or not in industrial settings, transportation, or smart houses, make a contribution actual-time statistics to virtual fashions, allowing higher tracking, predictive protection, and system optimization. This interconnectedness between the physical and digital worlds will continue to force innovation across various fields.

The capacity for virtual twins in schooling is also expanding. As digital environments emerge as extra interactive and immersive, instructional institutions can use digital twins to create digital simulations of complicated strategies, historical occasions, or medical phenomena. This makes gaining knowledge of extra engaging, dynamic, and experiential, permitting college students to have interaction with and discover subjects in approaches that were not formerly viable.

The broader societal and financial effect of digital twins cannot be overstated. The technology holds the capacity to increase productiveness, reduce operational expenses, and enhance high-quality across severa industries. With their capability to optimize approaches, lessen mistakes, and forecast capacity screw ups, virtual twins can drastically enhance operational efficiency in both private and public sectors. In the long term, the big adoption of digital twins may want to lead to massive financial boom and a more sustainable, efficient international economy.

Despite those promising tendencies, the whole potential of virtual twins remains unfolding. There are challenges to triumph over, specially round records safety, privacy, and moral considerations. As virtual twins turn out to be extra ubiquitous, the records they rely on ought to be protected to save you misuse and make certain the integrity of the systems they constitute. Additionally, the adoption of virtual twins would require sizable funding in infrastructure, generation, and talents improvement, as industries should put together their team of workers for the digital transformation that accompanies those improvements.

Looking beforehand, the future of virtual twins appears bright. With the ongoing evolution of device gaining knowledge of, AI, and sensor technologies, virtual twins are expected to grow to be even greater state-of-the-art and correct. The integration of those technologies will lead to more self sustaining systems, predictive analytics, and enhanced choice-making capabilities. The capability to simulate complex environments and take a look at new ideas in a danger-unfastened digital area will accelerate innovation and foster new answers to some of the arena's most pressing demanding situations.

The impact of digital twins extends past industry and commercial enterprise; they may essentially reshape how we interact with the world. From healthcare to urban making plans, virtual twins will enable greater personalised, green, and sustainable approaches of residing. As society moves closer to a extra virtual and interconnected destiny, the continued development of virtual twin era will play a crucial position in shaping the arena of day after today.

Digital twins represent a progressive step inside the evolution of digital technologies. Their significance lies now not handiest in their capacity to enhance overall performance, optimize structures, and reduce costs however additionally in their ability to create new opportunities for innovation and creativity throughout industries. As the generation continues to mature and combine with other emerging technology, the ability for virtual twins to transform the bodily and digital worlds will most effective continue to grow, marking a brand new technology in how we have interaction with and shape our surroundings.

12.2. Shaping the Future with Virtual Reality and Augmented Reality

Virtual reality (VR) and augmented reality (AR) are technology that have already started to seriously regulate the way we engage with the arena. As these technology preserve to evolve, they're poised to shape no longer most effective the future of leisure and gaming however also the methods wherein we work, learn, speak, and experience the sector round us. The ongoing advancements in VR and AR are unlocking a huge variety of opportunities, with profound implications for society, enterprise, schooling, healthcare, and past.

One of the maximum exciting aspects of VR and AR is their capability to blur the traces between the bodily and digital realms. Through immersive reviews, VR allows users to step into completely digital environments, whilst AR overlays digital elements onto the real world, improving the person's notion of their surroundings. This convergence of the bodily and digital worlds has extensive capacity, making an allowance for new types of interaction, verbal exchange, and creativity that had been formerly unattainable.

In training, VR and AR are reworking conventional learning studies by means of making them extra interactive, enticing, and handy. Virtual classrooms can provide students with immersive classes on everything from ancient events to scientific ideas, allowing them to revel in topics in ways that textbooks and lectures by myself cannot offer. AR can supplement physical learning environments by using offering real-time, interactive data approximately objects or places, assisting students benefit a deeper know-how of the material they are studying.

The integration of VR and AR into enterprise processes is also poised to revolutionize industries along with retail, real estate, healthcare, and design. For instance, in retail, virtual try-ons and augmented purchasing stories are allowing customers to look how merchandise might appearance in their houses or on their our bodies without needing to bodily engage with them. In real property, VR allows digital property tours, imparting potential customers with an immersive and sensible view of a assets while not having to go to in person. Healthcare experts are the usage of VR for education and simulations, enhancing their talents in a hazard-unfastened surroundings, while AR is being utilized in surgical procedures to offer actual-time facts and steering.

In the area of social interactions, VR and AR are reimagining the way we speak and collaborate. Virtual environments offer new systems for socializing, permitting people to have interaction in approaches that bridge geographical distances and create a experience of presence. With the upward thrust of social VR platforms, individuals can meet in virtual spaces, percentage experiences, or even collaborate on projects, as though they have been within the same room. For businesses, those technologies provide new opportunities for virtual meetings and collaboration, facilitating actual-time verbal exchange with colleagues, customers, and customers throughout the globe.

The leisure enterprise is one of the number one regions in which VR and AR have made their most superb effect. From immersive gaming reviews to interactive film reports, VR and AR are remodeling the way we enjoy content. VR permits gamers to enter game worlds and have interaction with them on a wholly new stage, whilst AR complements the gaming revel in with the aid of incorporating real-international factors into the virtual environment. In movie, VR and AR can offer visitors with interactive studies, wherein they can have an effect on the storyline or discover the film's environment in greater element. As technology improves, the immersive capacity of VR and AR in entertainment will continue to adapt, offering extra personalized and dynamic content material.

Moreover, the fast improvements in VR and AR are pushing the boundaries of human creativity. Artists, designers, and content material creators are the use of those technologies to create new forms of expression and storytelling. VR and AR provide modern methods to visualise and revel in art, permitting users to interact with and immerse themselves in innovative works. For instance, VR art installations allow humans to step inner a work of art, experiencing it from all angles and perspectives, whilst AR can add layers of virtual factors to bodily works of art, improving the viewer's enjoy.

The future of VR and AR also holds massive ability for healthcare, wherein those technology are being used to deal with patients in groundbreaking approaches. In mental fitness, VR is being utilized for cures inclusive of publicity remedy for tension issues, supporting sufferers confront their fears in a managed, virtual surroundings. AR is being utilized in scientific education and surgical procedures, imparting medical doctors actual-time, 3-d visualizations of a patient's anatomy or assisting them in complex tactics. As these technologies come to be greater included into healthcare, they could significantly enhance affected person effects and decorate the abilities of clinical professionals.

Looking toward the future, the ongoing improvement of VR and AR will cause even greater immersive and included studies. Advancements in hardware, such as lighter, extra comfortable headsets, will make these technologies extra available to a much wider target audience. The integration of AI, device getting to know, and 5G connectivity will allow more seamless and responsive interactions inside digital and augmented environments, bearing in mind extra fluid and lifelike reviews. As VR and AR technology emerge as more delicate and giant, they'll play an more and more important role in shaping the future of human interplay, mastering, creativity, and productiveness.

VR and AR are technology with the strength to reshape the world as we are aware of it. From revolutionizing industries to enhancing entertainment and social experiences, those technology provide a glimpse into a destiny where the limits between the physical and virtual worlds are increasingly more fluid. As VR and AR preserve to adapt, they may free up new opportunities for innovation, creativity, and human connection, ultimately reworking the way we stay, work, and interact with our surroundings. The destiny of VR and AR is one among boundless opportunities, with the ability to create a more immersive, connected, and dynamic international.

12.3. Future Trends and Expectations in Digital Twins

The future of digital twins holds monstrous promise as they preserve to evolve and influence a wide variety of industries. Initially rising in manufacturing and engineering, the scope of digital twins is expanding into areas together with healthcare, city planning, and environmental tracking. As generation advances, digital twins turns into even more included into both ordinary operations and contemporary improvements. The coming years will see a aggregate of technical advancements, more interoperability, and broader applications, remodeling how corporations and societies engage with the virtual and physical worlds.

One of the key developments shaping the future of virtual twins is the combination with advanced technologies along with artificial intelligence (AI), system gaining knowledge of (ML), and the Internet of Things (IoT). As these technology mature, digital twins could be capable of provide deeper insights, predictive analytics, and smarter decision-making skills. The mixture of AI and ML with digital twins will allow actual-time simulations, allowing structures to adapt autonomously to converting conditions and make predictions about destiny results. For instance, inside the car enterprise, virtual twins ought to enable self-studying structures that robotically adjust manufacturing traces to optimize performance or enhance vehicle protection capabilities based on actual-time records.

Another essential improvement can be the growing use of virtual twins in sectors past conventional industries. In healthcare, the capability to create personalised virtual twins of sufferers should cause greater accurate diagnoses, tailor-made treatments, and progressed affected person effects. These virtual fashions of character sufferers, produced from their genetic, scientific, and environmental information, may be used to simulate remedy responses and predict disorder progression, facilitating customized medication at an extraordinary level. Digital twins in healthcare may additionally extend to the modeling of whole healthcare systems, enabling higher aid allocation and management of public health crises.

Urban making plans and smart towns constitute another frontier for digital twins. As cities grow to be greater related and rely on smart technology for infrastructure control, virtual twins will play a pivotal position in making sure the efficiency and sustainability of city environments. Virtual representations of towns, complete with their visitors flows, power utilization, and environmental factors, will permit urban planners to test numerous eventualities and make statistics-driven selections approximately city improvement. This could considerably enhance the making plans of sustainable city spaces, reducing the environmental impact of fast urbanization and improving the first-rate of existence for residents.

In addition, the evolution of 5G and side computing will enable faster records processing and actual-time tracking, further improving the capabilities of virtual twins. The extended bandwidth supplied via 5G will allow for seamless transmission of huge quantities of facts, that is critical for creating actual-time, excessive-fidelity virtual twins. Edge computing will complement this by using processing information domestically on gadgets or close to the supply, reducing latency and enabling faster choice-making. This combination of technology will make digital twins even more effective in high-speed environments which include manufacturing, independent vehicles, and stay infrastructure monitoring.

Interoperability can also be a key element in the future of digital twins. As industries and sectors preserve to increase their digital twin technology independently, the need for seamless integration between distinctive structures will become important. The ability for digital twins to exchange facts across systems and industries will free up new possibilities for collaboration, improve the efficiency of go-zone operations, and result in more holistic solutions. For instance, a digital dual created for a manufacturing unit will be incorporated with the digital twin of the deliver chain, presenting a comprehensive view of manufacturing and logistics approaches and optimizing operations across the entire machine.

As virtual twins emerge as more and more on hand and big, they'll also end up extra person-friendly, permitting a broader variety of customers—from small corporations to authorities groups—to harness their potential. The democratization of digital dual technology will open up possibilities for innovation in diverse fields, making it less difficult for agencies of all sizes to integrate digital twins into their operations. Cloud-based totally solutions and software-as-a-carrier (SaaS) models will decrease the boundaries to entry, permitting companies without significant technical understanding to take benefit of virtual dual generation.

Looking ahead, virtual twins will preserve to power the adoption of extra sustainable practices, specially in industries consisting of electricity, production, and production. Virtual modeling can assist minimize waste and enhance resource efficiency, at the same time as also allowing groups to are expecting the environmental impact of their operations. In energy, digital twins may be used to simulate renewable electricity systems, optimizing the era, garage, and distribution of power. Similarly, in construction, digital twins can simulate constructing designs to make sure electricity efficiency, assisting to fulfill worldwide sustainability desires.

The future of digital twins may even involve extra use of immersive technologies such as virtual fact (VR) and augmented fact (AR) to have interaction with and visualize digital dual fashions. The combination of virtual twins with VR and AR will permit for more intuitive, immersive, and interactive methods to explore and manage virtual models, improving collaboration, education, and design processes. For example, engineers and architects ought to use AR glasses to overlay actual-time statistics from a digital dual onto bodily objects, offering instant insights and facilitating selection-making immediately.

The future of virtual twins is filled with potential, pushed with the aid of the integration of AI, ML, IoT, and other superior technologies. These digital fashions will become more specific, responsive, and ubiquitous, with packages extending a long way beyond traditional industries. As the skills of virtual twins keep growing, they will play a critical role in shaping industries, city areas, healthcare structures, and our broader societal systems. The convergence of bodily and digital worlds thru digital twins will redefine how we control, optimize, and innovate in almost each factor of modern-day existence. The opportunities are giant, and the destiny of virtual twins guarantees to transform the way we have interaction with each the real and digital worlds.